A Funny Thing Happened on the Way to a Funeral

James Auchmuty

Parson's Porch Books

www.parsonsporchbooks.com

A Funny Thing Happened on the Way to a Funeral

ISBN: Softcover 978-1-949888-11-9

Copyright © 2018 by James Auchmuty

All rights reserved. No part of this book may be reproduced or transmitted in any form or by any means, electronic or mechanical, including photocopying, recording, or by any information storage and retrieval system, without permission in writing from the publisher.

A Funny Thing Happened on the Way to a Funeral

Contents

Foreword 9
My First Funeral 11
All Things Work Together 13
A Memorable Moment in The Sun 14
Advanced Planning 16
A First Time, Up Close Look at Death 17
A Left-Handed Compliment 19
A "Hats On" Tribute 20
To Timon with Sympathy 22
An Ethnic First 24
All Is Well That Ends Well 26
Gender Crisis 28
Hope 29
My Most Unusual Funeral 30
Honoring the Dead 32
Just Call Aubie 34
I'll Fly Away 35
Identity in Question 36
I'll Fly Away II 38
John Wesley's Lengthened Shadow 39
Left High and Dry 40
Men Need Not Apply 42
Mistaken Identity 43
No Love Lost 44
North, East, South, West 45
Overcoming Stress 47
Old Men 49
On Saying Good Bye 51
Proceed with Caution 53

Paradigm Shifts 54
Peace in The Valley 56
Prophecy or Curse? 57
Piety Personified 58
Roller Coaster 59
Remarks at Memorial Service and Marker Dedication for Christy Murphy 60
Surprise! 63
Think You've Heard It All? 65
To Err Is Human 66
The Death of a President 68
The Body: Whole or Parts 70
The Amputee 71
The Exorcism 72
Equal Representation 74
The New Columbarium 76
The Will of God 78
Taps: An Encore 80
The WORD 81
The Patriot in Short Pants 83
Unwanted Visitors 84
Unwanted Still Born 86
It is Well with My Soul 87
Did You Ever Think When the Hearse Went By…? 89
We Preach Our Own Funeral 91
Weighty Matters 93
Who Will Guard the Guard? 94
Where There Is A Will 95
Obits 96
More Obits 98

Last of Last Words	100
A Miracle	102
A Sibling Relationship as Cold as the Corpse	104
Adios	106
An Overstated Demise	107
A Kaleidoscope of Death	108
B as In Bitter Cold and Brevity	109
Bargain Basement Burials	110
B.J.	112
Circus	114
Contrasts	116
Comfort	118
Christmas Sorrow	119
DR. JOHN: Scholar, Teacher, Farmer, Friend	120
Drugs: A Grave Issue	122
Flexibility	124
Family Feud	126
Face Card	128
An Unclaimed Blessing	129
Asian Mantra	131
A Rare Flash of Insight	132
Things Are Not Always as They Seem	133
Above or Beneath the Sod	134
Quo Vadis?	135
When Heaven Becomes Hell	136
Block 30	137
Letting "Pass Away" Pass Away	138

Foreword

There's a double sadness to funerals. Most Americans have never ridden in a limousine before, until they're in one following a hearse that's carrying a relative who has never received flowers before.
~Robert Orben~

A Funny Thing Happened on the Way to A Funeral may seem inappropriate as the title of a book that talks about deaths and burials. But as a former teacher astutely observed, words have uses rather than meanings. Funny is one of those words. Something may be funny/ha-ha—amusing, humorous or funny/odd—unusual, out of the ordinary, even weird. And there are times when a thing is simultaneously funny/ha ha and funny/odd.

My experience across more than sixty years of ministry has included all three uses, and that fact began early. Though a Baptist, I began like a Methodist serving a circuit of two rural churches. They referred to me as their pastor, but I was more like what the Air National Guard calls a "week-end warrior." I was a college student in Birmingham, the churches were 120 miles away in Chambers County, and I had no car when the first one called me. One met on first and third Sundays, the other on second and fourth Sundays. On fifth Sundays I went hungry! And to keep things interesting, though the churches were in the same Alabama county, one operated on central time and the other on eastern.

I discovered this pattern applied in ministering to those who were genuinely grieved as well as to those, to put it nicely, "less emotionally stressed"; of whom there are many. Moods and happenings have run the gamut from: pious to secular; heart-breaking to funny bone-tickling; sublime to ridiculous; holy to irreverent. *A Funny Thing Happened on The Way to A Funeral*, therefore, seemed most appropriate as a title.

I also have included snippets from, facts about and full obituaries unrelated to the stories that follow the funny/odd sequence. Sadly, for many, the obituary may be the only time a person's name ever appears in the newspaper; they do not get to see it for they must have died for it to appear; and if that were not enough, the family must have paid a fee for the printing of the announcement. And to add to the irony, the obituary must have met the paper's *dead*line.

The examples also show: (1) Perhaps due to spell-check on computers, proofreaders—like dinosaurs, dial phones and diapers made of real cloth—are a thing of the past. (2) Spell-check is no match for those tricky homophones, words that sound alike but are spelled differently. (3) Mark Twain never was more correct, "The difference in the right word and the almost right word is the difference between lightning and lightning bug."

I put this material in print at the encouragement of funeral professionals, those in academe, colleagues in ministry and friends. These all are true-life episodes that show: truth is stranger than fiction; occasionally it is very difficult to keep a straight face; and ministers may not be as straight-laced and insulated from the real world as many might think—or for good guilty reasons—might hope.

My First Funeral

The deceased had spent most of her adult life in a distant facility equipped to handle her disability. The family was more relieved than grieved when she died. Not I!! This being my first funereal to conduct would have been traumatic enough, but. ....

Two days before, one of my prominent front teeth—not quite Bugs Bunny size, but close—was knocked out in a basketball game leaving only a stump projecting near the gum line. (Afterward, I went by the dorm to pick up my date. I greeted her with a broad smile, and she nearly fainted.) The dentist did prep work for a permanent crown and then rifled the contents of a cigar box in search of a temporary. Not quite battleship gray in color, it was crooked and considerably shorter than the one it replaced. Concerned about how I might look and how I would speak, as though the obvious could be hidden, I was a basket case the entire 120-mile trip from the campus to the church.

When I met with the family, I was informed that they had also enlisted a second preacher, a seasoned minister from a church in town who held an earned doctorate. I thought there is a God after all, but my pious exuberance was short-lived. It evaporated like the foam on a shaken soft drink when they quickly added, "He will assist you!"

Whatever transpired apparently did not reach the level of an offense that merited being fired. I have no idea what I said, nor how stupid I looked conducting that service. Though I stood in the pulpit, faced the congregation, read Scripture and uttered some remarks, I dared not move my upper lip. My primary prayer was not for those in the pews laying their loved one to rest, rather my prayer was for me: "Lord put your arms around my shoulders and put your hand over my mouth!"

All Things Work Together

While shopping on a Saturday morning at Big Lots in Pelham, Alabama, my cell phone rang. In the words of Yogi Berra, it was "Deja vu all over again". The failure of someone to enlist a minister was discovered only ninety minutes before funeral time.

I was sympathetic, but explained I was 12 miles from home, in a jogging suit, and then would have a 22-mile trip to the funeral home.

"You've got to do it. We will play taped music until you get here. Come on!"

Fortunately, I had showered earlier, traffic was light, and the police were on coffee break, likely at the donut shop. I arrived safely without a speeding ticket, and the service began only 15 minutes late.

The driver of the flower truck took full advantage of my tardiness. During the wait, he had sweet talked the daughter of the deceased into a date for square dancing the next night.

Some apparently process their grief more quickly than others.

A Memorable Moment in The Sun

Funeral directors seem more interested in the weather than Jim Cantore of the Weather Channel or any of the ubiquitous local meteorologists. Seldom is the question, "Will it be hot or cold?" but "How hot or how cold will it be?" The wide-open spaces of cemeteries are known for attracting equatorial and polar extremes.

This July day began hotter than usual, even for a mid-summer Alabama day. As the temperature continued its rapid climb toward the century mark, it was as if one had gone from an electric blanket to a microwave oven.

As the crowd gathered, I stood off to the side, away from the tent, talking to the director. He is a rather rotund, good-humored black man whose head is as void of hair as a peeled onion. But for complexion, he might have starred as Kojak in the lead role of "Digger O'Dell, the Friendly Undertaker". Sweat —perspiration on steroids—already had bled through the coat of his navy blue suit causing it to stick to his back as though he were a contestant in a wet T shirt contest. With the ambidexterity of a professional basketball player, he had a full-time job mopping his pate and brow, first with his right hand and then with his left.

Minutes before the service began a man showed up wearing a straw hat, the brim of which seemed as wide as an opened umbrella, a gringo version of the "Frito Bandito." Pointing to that man, I said, "David, would you like me to go over and see if I can borrow that hat for you?" Breaking out with a broad grin so characteristic of him, he said, "That might not be a bad idea, because I don't need no more tan."

Advanced Planning

The business card of a local mortuary/cemetery representative lists his name followed by his job description that leaves little in doubt: "Pre-need planning before the need." Making such plans of death has many advantages. The individual is assured that he/she will get what they want; decisions can be made rationally rather than emotionally; and survivors are spared the frustration of having to do so many things and go so many places in such a short time.

One of our church members accompanied her mother for such a purpose. With all the insurance policies and other needed papers in order, it was time to talk money. Goods and services were priced individually. Things went well until they came to the line item "hairdresser... $50.00." The mother, who came of age during the Great Depression, protested at such an "outrageous price." She said, "Let's just eliminate that." Daughter and director reminded her that she would want to look her best and how her hair looked would play a great part in that.

The arguments go nowhere. Then in desperation and disgust, the daughter asked, "Well, Mother, what do you want me to do when that time comes?" In a voice of calm resolve came the answer, "I'll just have it fixed before I come down here."

A First Time, Up Close Look at Death

The doctor from the near-by town arrived at the tiny, rural home shortly after I. The small, oscillating fan brought no relief to the near-stifling heat, and his words brought no comfort to the sick man's handicapped daughter, the two neighbors or me. "He won't last long. There is nothing else I can do for him, so I am going back to town. When the time comes call Mr. Sanders at the funeral home." Within 30 minutes the words of the physician-turned-prophet came to fulfillment.

After the phone call, the daughter said, "Jim, would you go in the kitchen and get Papa's teeth for me? They are in the pie safe in a mug." She was on target. They were in the pie safe in a mug that once was home to A & P brand peanut butter. What had been water covering the teeth had turned into a sickening, cucumber green crud about two inches thick. The store-bought choppers had been out of service so long I was convinced the man could have cracked "hiker" nuts with his gums!

By the grace of God, I was able to suppress my nausea, and holding the mug at maximum arm's length, I returned to the bedroom. No sooner than I had set the vessel on the bedside table than the daughter said to me, "Would you put them in for me?" My first impulse was to have them call Mr. Sanders back and tell him to bring two cots, for I thought I was going to die. I assured her Mr. Sanders was a professional and would be there in only a matter of minutes. (I would not have attempted to extract, extricate or excavate those teeth with a pair of long handled, needle-nose pliers.)

How I arrived safely at home still boggles my mind. I drove those 15 miles through the back woods faster than usual, and certain someone was following, I looked more in the rearview mirror than through the windshield. Once there, sleep was more successful fleeing me than I was fleeing the ghost of the first person I had ever seen die. Sick to my stomach and frightened out of my mind that was one of the longest nights of my life.

A Left-Handed Compliment

I do not do long funeral services and I do not do tear-jerkers. Because I do not know most of these people, I have tried to develop an air-tight, one-size-fits-all approach. Being a Baptist, there is no prescribed order that must be followed, so I talk about remembering the deceased, inventorying our own lives and connecting with the good resources of God, using familiar (at least to some) favorite passages of Scripture that focus on strength, courage and Christian hope. I always stress no one preaches another's funeral. That is a task each does daily, and the content of that sermon is determined by: one's relationship to God through Christ, the uses one makes of his/her time, talent, influence and money; the causes one serves; and the investments one makes with his/her love.

Lou, a local auto mechanic, apparently was accustomed to ministers, taking full advantage of their captive audience, never passing up the opportunity to tilt the scales in favor of their own denomination which always seemed to hold the exclusive franchise to Heaven. That he found missing in my approach in both services he attended that I officiated.

After the second one, he came to me afterward and said, "Reverend, I kinda' like the way you preach funerals. You don't stress no particular kind of religion."

A "Hats On" Tribute

Looking over the congregation that filled the house I might have assumed I was attending the Kentucky Derby; every female, old and young, was wearing a hat. But this was a church not Churchill Downs, and this was a funeral not a horse race. The scene was fitting for one who had been a millinery shopkeeper's dream, a woman whose hat collection numbered more than three hundred.

My maternal grandmother, who believed in "marking babies," would have explained that hobby this way. Every pregnant woman should be careful of what she looked at, because what she saw could impact the infant's looks, likes and character. That being the case, the mother of the deceased must have been a devoted fan of Hedda Hopper.

One day Julia Alice called my wife and me over to talk about plans for her funeral. She wanted Sue's opinion on which hat best matched her "shroud," a bright pink dress. "You know I always wore a hat to church, and I am sure taking one with me when I go to heaven." And she said her collection would be on display at the church the day of her funeral. Every woman and girl was to select one as a keepsake and wear it during the service. The variety of headgear ranged in style from pill boxes that looked like inverted bird's nests to plumed wide-breams that resembled golf umbrellas on Weight Watchers.

The eulogy would be built around hats symbolizing the roles she played in life: wife, mother, grandmother, educator, deaconess, churchlady and the local version of Kathryn Tucker Windham, the state's legendary reader-story teller.

Immediately following the "Amen," the ladies were asked to occupy the center section of the sanctuary for a group picture. The photo was as beautiful in color as any spring scene in the Botanical Gardens.

The service was different to be sure, but it was a most appropriate "Hats On" tribute to one affectionately known to her church family as "the hat lady."

To Timon with Sympathy

To "scare away evil spirits," the black-clad, male corpse wore a rawhide necklace that featured a dried bat pendant. His matching, western-style Stetson hat rested on the pillow beside his head—at least for the time being. Immediately before the casket was closed the hat was to be placed over his face. And in an apparent "you can take it with you" scheme, a backpack containing all his belongings, along with his boots, also were to be placed in the casket.

Burial was in a rural cemetery atop a beautiful, sloping knoll. The grave was dug parallel to a fence that separated burial ground from pasture. Because of the slope, chairs for the family were placed at the foot of the casket, and they sat slightly tilted at a backward angle.

Rather than simply taking a chair on the front row in a normal fashion, the father of the deceased plopped down as if he had been shot. Immediately he tumbled backward into the second row of seats, his legs waving in the air like arms at a Bill Gaither concert. Trying to cushion the fall, he grabbed a handful of the barbed wire fence which cut his fingers and tore his jacket. Once upright and laughing he said, "That's the reason I didn't wear my best suit." (At that point the funeral director cancelled his cell phone call to the corporate lawyer.)

Filling the grave was delayed while the father retrieved five Walmart tote bags from his car. He then neatly placed the contents on the lid of the vault—thirty small packages securely wrapped in freezeproof paper as if from the distribution center of Omaha Steaks. This was his son's collection of frozen ferrets!

On the return trip to town, I imagined a tearful cast on the set of *The Lion King* joining Timon as he grieved the deaths of his distant cousins.

An Ethnic First

Given the perceived differences in culture, religious expression and worship style, little did I know what to expect when called upon to conduct my first funeral for an African-American person. The deceased was retired from the railroad. Now a widower, he had been married for more than 40 years. He was a stickler for education. He put his 2 daughters, both now public school teachers, through college.

The women were well groomed, quite well-dressed, and very articulate. They wanted a simple, Christian funeral for their beloved dad. They would leave the details up to me with one exception. I was to read a poem their father had written.

I need God; indeed, I do.
I need Him to see me through.
Every day and every hour
I need his sustaining power.

Even today I wonder what may have inspired those words. Was he passed over for a job in the days of Jim Crow? Did he suffer some injustice in society that could have turned him against the world? Whatever the reason, he found in the good resources of God coping power to meet, prevail and overcome.

I keep a copy of his poem in my notebook and in my head. Often, I use these words as a call to prayer in both worship and funeral services. Those lines are a constant reminder of my own dependence on and indebtedness to the love and grace of

God who made all of us, and whose continued Presence with us we know as Holy Spirit.

All Is Well That Ends Well

Jimbo and I were cutting two long rows of shrubbery that flanked property lines and we were pruning crepe myrtle limbs as big as baseball bats when my phone rang. It was 1:08 pm. A call to 911 could not have sounded more urgent. A funeral already had begun at a church, and through someone's negligence, no pallbearers had been enlisted.

"Tell me there is some way you can get 4 pallbearers to the cemetery ASAP!"

"Donna, we are cutting bushes. We are wearing old jeans, sweat shirts and toboggans trying to keep warm. I don't see..."

"I don't care what you look like," she interrupted, "just have 4 warm bodies there."

I called Bill at home, and Jimbo caught Hubert at a credit union. Both said they were leaving right then to head that way.

The well-to-do family in shiny, expensive cars arrived in procession. They were accommodated by four Episcopal priests in their finest vestments. And there we were looking as if the mortuary staff had enlisted homeless guys who live in cardboard boxes under the I-20/I-459 viaduct to serve as pallbearers.

The next week the director reported, "You won't believe this about that funeral the other day. That family was thrilled. The deceased formerly had owned a construction company and they believed he would have been gratified to have employee look-alikes serve as his pallbearers."

Gender Crisis

Three side-by-side doors flanked the hallway leading to the chapel of the former Angwin's Mortuary in Ensley. They were identical except for signage: Ladies; Gentlemen; Ministers.

Completing my visit with the family I had come to see, I approached the receptionist's desk and in a rather firm tone said, "I'd like to speak with the manager!" Little did I know he was a man from my home town that I had not seen in 20 years. After recalling old times, the conversation took on a new twist.

"James," I said, "I want to talk to you about this third gender business. According to your signs, folk in my profession are neither female nor male but a third breed of cat. What's the deal?"

He appeared stunned and shocked.

"And if that were not enough," I continued, "You don't even think we have the same plumbing configuration as the other two. Out of curiosity I went in the room marked Ministers and the only thing in there is a desk."

By now he realizes I am playing him along. And after a bit more conversation I ended the visit with a good bye and some good advice. "Good to see you again, my man. And if I were you, I'd be very careful in opening the top, right-hand drawer of that desk."

Hope

As if Providence were smiling on us, the grave was dug under the canopy of a big oak's long branches, the only shade in that cemetery that looked as if it had been a cow pasture in its former life. A small gathering of family and friends gathered around that rectangular hole dug six feet in the earth's crust.

After most of the crowd had disappeared, the daughter of the deceased called the director aside, spoke in a low voice and handed him two items to be placed in the casket—a pack of cigarettes and a BIC lighter. She said it would please her dad because, "He was never without one."

On the way back to the funeral home the director said, "Placing objects in the casket is not unheard of, but it is unusual."

I replied that I saw it in a different light. "I saw it as an expression of hope."

"How in the world do you figure that?" he asked.

"What did you place in the casket?"

"You know what it was. You saw it," he responded in an almost aggravated tone.

"The key was not in the pack of smokes, but in the lighter. The fact she included the BIC was a sure sign she didn't believe there was any fire in the place her father had gone."

My Most Unusual Funeral

The homeless man with his tattered cardboard, crudely lettered sign that asked for food had taken his position at the junction of a busy surface street and a ramp to I-65. As the driver of a tractor-trailer turned onto the ramp the right back wheels of his rig ran over and killed the beggar he had just helped.

The funeral was scheduled for Monday afternoon. Within an hour, the day had been changed from Monday to Sunday. That meant the funeral of this homeless man would cost an additional $400.00, the cemetery's surcharge for weekend interment. A grand total of three attended, and like the partisan division in Congress, two from the family sat on one side of the aisle and the best friend of the deceased on the other side.

As we were leaving the grave, the best friend asked me, "Have we had the funeral yet?" When I assured him, we had both a chapel and graveside committal, he responded, "Well, what they going to do now?" I explained as best I could the lowering of the casket, the placing of the vault lid and covering the grave with dirt.

As he turned the ignition in his car, a collection of Ford, Chevrolet and Chrysler parts that resembled Joseph's coat of many colors (Genesis 37)—a familiar click-click sound was heard. Battery trouble!

Before anyone could get battery cables, he had raised his trunk lid and brought out a claw hammer and a large nail. He drove the nail into a battery terminal, turned the ignition, and miraculously it cranked.

In a contest of "My Most Unusual Funerals," this one, from start to finish, would certainly be named to the Queen's Court of Honor.

Honoring the Dead

Plagiarism is borrowing another's thoughts, idea or language without giving them proper credit; give them credit and it is called research! In our church we use the term "baptizing" for both categories.

To honor those members who had died within the last calendar year, we acknowledged "baptizing" ideas from Memorial Day, All Saints Day, Decoration Day, Easter and some area churches, without citing which came from where. Among other things, the name of each decedent would be called; the family recognized and presented a flower in honor of their loved one.

Lynda, the church secretary, was assigned procuring the flowers and bud vases. I suggested carnations, an idea she quickly vetoed.

"No way!" Lynda said.

I asked, "Why not? They are appropriate and are less expensive than roses."

"I'm ordering roses," she said in a matter-of-fact tone. "Carnations smell too much like a funeral."

Aspiring to become mayor of a Birmingham suburb, the manager of the local funeral home had placed one of his red, white and blue campaign signs on the lawn of the building. No funeral attendee could miss it, and it was easily read by those passing by on that busy street. It surely caught my eye.

I had known the man for some time, and no sooner had known I entered the building he called me aside. Though the sign was strategically located for high visibility, he apparently had some guarded concerns about the propriety of the placement of electioneering material at a place that served what some theologians call the "elect" and "non-elect" alike. "What do you think?" he asked. "Do you think it is okay?"

I remembered that bit folk wisdom which says, "Most of the time someone asks for your opinion, they don't want your opinion, they are looking for a response that will re-enforce the decision they already have made." He really wanted the office, he was manager of the business, apparently the placement the placard was not violation of city code or company policy, and I did not live within the corporate limits. So, rather than rain on his parade by expressing how undignified and out of place it seemed to me, I said, "I think it is a great idea," words spoken with fingers crossed but which made him smile. "Are you serious?" he asked excitedly. "Yes. Most appropriate. The dead in this town have been voting for a hundred years."

Whether it was the influence of the sign or the truth of my observation, he was elected and is now in his third term! And who knows where it will end? Perhaps, like that Chicago congressman, he will want to be buried in the district that elected him, so that he, too might "continue to be active in politics."

Just Call Aubie

The setting was inside a funeral home, but it looked for the world like a pre-Harvey Updike scene on Toomer's Corner after an Auburn football victory.

Long strips of toilet tissue hung from the branches of the potted plants in the foyer.

School colors were featured in memorabilia displayed on tables as well as in the floral arrangements. The funeral directors, pall bearers and many of the attendees wore orange and blue ties.

An eagle was featured on the cover of the program. Inside, instead of a usual brief obituary, the Auburn Creed was printed.

The service closed with the people being asked to stand for the playing of—you guessed it—"War Eagle," the fight song of the university located on "the loveliest village on the plains."

That day I was a bit ill-at-ease. I felt more like Aubie presiding at a pep rally than a Christian minister conducting a funeral.

I'll Fly Away

"A graveside service with a ceremonial white dove release creates a beautiful moment of silence at any funeral or memorial where all one can hear is the gentle sounds of white wings against the air. A flock of White Doves are released, while one is held back for a moment for a family member to release. As the doves circle above like angels in a breath-taking formation, the single white dove ascends to join the flock, as if angels were escorting it off to heaven. This makes a heartfelt and symbolic conclusion to your loved one's memorial or funeral ceremony." (Alabama White Doves).

The White Dove Release Society emphasizes proper care and safety of these birds, which really are homing pigeons (aka Rock Doves). They will not be released in heavy rain, in the dark and only outside that offers a view to the sky.

All went well at one service at Elmwood Cemetery until the solo bird was released. It had hardly reached the height of 10 feet when, instead of joining the flock serving as angelic escorts to heaven, it was met by a hungry hawk that took it to the ground and dismembered it. Instead of the silence promised in the ad, the horrified family heard instead the crunching of bones and what they saw was the flying of feathers.

Since this releasing practice is built solely on symbolism, dare one ask what this strange turn of events suggested about the spirit of the deceased?

Identity in Question

"Be sure to get here early because the family wants to talk to you about their mother." And, that I was.

I met the son and daughter immediately upon arriving, but no sooner than we had said hello, the son rejoined a group with whom he had been talking. The sister was helpful, but she was insistent that I talk further with her brother.

At five minutes before the service, Mr. Social Butterfly decided he could spare the time for conversation. It took him only 5 words to tell me the facts without which I would be greatly incapacitated in the execution of my responsibility. He said, "Mama didn't want no preaching."

The adage says, "Speech is silver, but silence is golden." True, but sometimes silence is plain yellow! I wanted to say, "Why in God's name did you enlist a minister if that is the case? Why did you not get a game warden, butcher or hairdresser?" But I didn't.

I followed my normal pattern, and afterward the Social Butterfly said to me, "You did a good job."

Of course, I was pleased that he was pleased, but my identity, if not calling, became a question in my own mind. At a service several months prior, a man had told me he liked the way I conducted funerals because I "didn't stress no particular religion." Now this. If "Mama didn't want no preaching," and what I did was satisfactory, how would you classify what I said?

Time answers many philosophical questions, and soon I was at peace with myself again, my identity intact!

I'll Fly Away II

The husband, numbed by the death of his dear wife, was unaware of the presence of two others who now stood by his side. At length he turned toward the director and me and nodded, as if to grant us permission to speak. After the introductions he turned and resumed his stare at the lovely lady in the casket.

"Sir," I said, "I would like to make this service as personal as I can, so I would appreciate any information that would help me with that. Is there something special about her you would like mentioned?"

Never looking up he said bluntly, "To tell you the truth, she wanted to be reincarnated as a bird."

The small group in attendance occupied the front pews (proving beyond a doubt they were not Baptists). The funeral director was seated in the back near the door and register stand. As I took my position at the podium, the director stood, folded his arms and began flapping them as though they were wings!

Had he played a tape of "I'll Fly Away," there would have been another funeral. His!

John Wesley's Lengthened Shadow

I never advanced beyond the Tenderfoot rank in Boy Scouts, but I have found their motto helpful, "Be prepared." As one who does services for folk of all denominations, my library includes copies of traditional services of these respective traditions.

This day I was to be a Methodist by request of the family coming in from out of town. When I met them, I made sure I was holding against my chest a book bound in black with its gold lettered title prominently showing, <u>RITUAL: THE METHODIST CHURCH</u>.

At the graveside, I thought I would go the "second mile" to remove any lingering doubt about my credentials. I closed my remarks by saying, "As Wesley was fond of saying, 'The best part of it all is God is with us.'"

After the benediction a man who had been seated on the second row of those dreadfully, uncomfortable folding chairs—always placed too close together— virtually climbed over the first row, fortunately not breaking a leg, embraced me in a bear hug and said, "It is so-o-o good to hear a Methodist preacher. No 'ole Baptist would ever quote Wesley."

I left with a real sense of security certain I had not fallen from grace.

Left High and Dry

"Is this Mr. Auchmuty?" the man on the telephone asked?

"Yes," I replied.

"This is Sgt. Morris from the Jefferson County coroner's office. Do you know a Miss Janice Smith?"

I replied, "Yes, she is our church secretary."

Sgt. Morris said, "She has just been killed in a car wreck. Your business card was in her purse, and that's why I am calling you. Do you happen to know any of her family?"

"I have met her sister."

Then Sgt. Morris said, "I have had 3 death calls in the last few hours. I wonder if I could ask you to contact that sister for me?"

I told him, "She lives in Mount Olive. That is 30 miles from here, and I don't have a clue what her address is. But, if you will have a deputy meet me at the First Baptist Church and take me to the sister's house, I will be glad to help."

The deputy took me to the house, and as it turned out, he knew the sister and her husband. He knocked, the husband answered, and the officer said, "This is the preacher and he needs to talk to you."

The couple replied, "We're busy and don't have time for that."

"But this is important," the deputy added.

The husband opened the door and invited us in. I was first to enter. When I looked back, the deputy was already in his car. His tire marks no doubt are still in that drive way. He was off as if to a national nuclear emergency or was doing a practice run for the weekend drag race.

The guys with badges may be brave in situations where guns, billy sticks and Mace are needed. But when it comes to emotional toughness, some at least, are as weak as the rest of us.

Men Need Not Apply

An unmarried woman in her seventies, a member of the church, had spent her adult life as caretaker for ailing, aging parents and as a rescue mission for nieces with children whose marriages had unraveled. That meant the gas tank of her social life perpetually ran on empty.

She dropped in and asked that I make her an ironclad promise. "I want you to promise me without fail that you will have 6 female pallbearers for my funeral." Assuming she was joking, I said, "Oh, sure!" Sensing my mood, she let me know in no uncertain terms she was dead serious (no pun intended). "Why?" I asked. She was quick to reply, "No man has ever carried me out in life, and I'm be damned if one is going to carry me out in death!"

Mistaken Identity

The speed of the car carrying five teenagers was too much to make the sharp curve. The vehicle left the road, turned over and came to rest upside down in a culvert.

The sole survivor, clinging to life, was rushed to a trauma unit where shocked parents and friends kept an anxious vigil.

In the meantime, parents of one of the victims gathered at the funeral home. She and the survivor were best of friends, looked alike and often shared clothes and jewelry. During the private viewing time for the family, the mother noticed the ears of the lifeless child that lay before them were double-pierced. Her daughter's ears had only one piercing. This was not their daughter!

When the mistaken identity was discovered, the family that had been at the funeral home rushed to the hospital. And the family that had been at the hospital slowly made their way to the funeral home.

The victim and her family were members of the church I served. I had baptized her. And now I had the sad, difficult assignment of speaking at her funeral.

That multi-fatality accident and the accompanying unusual turn of events left the entire community stunned and in shocked disbelief. To provide for a time of collective grieving and attempting to bring some sense of closure, the high school sponsored a memorial service for all four students. And I was asked to lead that service.

No Love Lost

Unlike anything I had ever seen, a four-foot, chain link fence split the church cemetery into two equal parts. It is a testimony to the social and caste divisions within the congregation. Members of the family who gave the land on which the church is built and for whom the church is named, the haves, are buried on the left side of that barricade made of woven steel. The lesser breeds are buried on the right.

The church was united, however, in its dislike for the new suburban neighborhoods that now complete surround this once semi-rural congregation. And the neighborhood has responded in kind. That became billboard evident during my third funeral there.

The small crowd had gathered for the graveside service—on the right-hand side of the fence of course. As the burial rites were about to begin, the woman living adjacent to the church decided she needed to trim her manicured lawn. The proximity of the mower's roar drowned out the preacher's words. Suddenly, a kinsman of the deceased angrily made his way to the property line. A man who apparently learned to whisper at a saw mill, addressed the culprit in a demanding, stentorian tone reminiscent of Reagan's demand of Gorbachev to "tear down that wall,", shouted, "Shut that g-- d--- thing off! We are trying to have a funeral over here!"

North, East, South, West

The once rural cemetery had long since been surrounded by urban sprawl, but it still operated as if change never had taken place. Decoration Day, that Sunday in May when sales of plastic flowers warm the hearts and fill the coffers of the Taiwanese, is still a not-to-be-messed-with honored tradition. And at least one of the volunteer committee is present whenever there is a burial.

The pallbearers had placed the casket on the lowering device exactly as they had been instructed, the service had been concluded, and the crowd had dispersed when one of the professional grave-diggers began asking for help from the few stragglers who remained.

He said the casket's position should be reversed in keeping with the tradition of burying the corpse facing east, the direction of sun rise. I and one other volunteered to help, but more hands would be welcome.

"Aren't you going to help us?" the digger asked the elderly committee member in charge.

"Nope," came the reply.

"Come on man, we need you!"

"Nope, 'cause I believe if God is strong enough to raise you up, he is strong enough to turn you around."

"My kind of man!" I said. And to this day I believe I heard my back say, "Amen."

Overcoming Stress

Preachers like most folk, welcome calls in the middle of the night with the same degree of enthusiasm as a call from the IRS saying, "You are being audited."

The phone awakened me around 2 A.M. I fully expected some member of the congregation had gone the way of all the earth.

"Preacher, I'm getting married."

"Congratulations."

"I am getting married tonight and I want you to marry us."

About as incensed as a bear aroused half way through hibernation, I said, "One, I am not marrying you tonight, and I bet you don't have a license."

"A license? You have to have a license to get married?"

"Yes, you must have a license. It's a state law."

"Ain't there something you could say to make it legal tonight?"

Decades later I was asked to conduct that man's funeral. His church was without a pastor and my schedule would allow it, so in a weak moment, I agreed. He had become overly friendly with Jim Beam and had dwindled away to skin and bones.

A few tearless friends and his only surviving relative gathered at the grave. I was bodily present, but my mind was riveted on a phone call that I had received years earlier at an ungodly hour.

I made some remarks I thought appropriate, read some Scripture and had a prayer. It was extremely difficult, but I managed to keep a straight face. In the handling of that stress, my stress was the exact opposite of his when he made that call: reason prevailed over desire.

And I hope he had made better plans for the Great Beyond than he did for his wedding.

Old Men

Clad in wrinkled clothes, his shirt tail out, stubble beard, disheveled hair, his sockless feet having made cuffs out of wingtip shoes, the old gentleman could have sat for the portrait of "basket case." Married more than 60 years, childless, and with no extended family, he had been his incapacitated wife's around-the-clock caretaker for the past eleven years. Now she was dead. Feeling lost and alone, he paced the lobby of the mortuary much like expectant fathers are known to do. As he moved back and forth across the room, he kept repeating in a loud voice, "I need someone to talk to Jesus for me. I need someone to talk to Jesus for me."

I went to him as quickly as I could upon completing an assignment with another family. I invited him to sit, but he was too restless. He poured out his heart as I listened, and then looking me straight in the eye, "I need someone to talk to Jesus for me." Choking back my own tears, I put my arm around his shoulder and there in that lobby, with people coming and going to two other services, I did the best I could to be his priest. I talked to Jesus for him.

Mr. Watt widowed after nearly 65 years of marriage and now largely deserted by his next of kin, two nephews, lived down the farm-to-market road about a mile past the church. I preached in his rural, crossroads community, twice a month. I usually visited him on one of those trips. We usually sat on the porch talking for a while, me the 20-year-old preacher in slacks, short sleeve shirt and tie and he in his "over-hauls and flannel shirt". Each time I heard his life's story and each time he would apologize for being unable to "make preaching." But to assure me it was well with his soul, he would always say "I listen to the 'Truck' Wagon Gang every Sunday morning." (The Chuck Wagon Gang was a southern gospel quartet widely popular in the 1950's.)

I would then help him to my car, and after a two-mile ride, we would come to the cemetery located across the road from Bethel church. With the old-fashioned brush broom he kept nearby, he would sweep clean the sandy earth that covered the grave of his dear wife. With that, he would sit on a bench, we would cry together, and then make our way back to the humble little house he called home where the silence was seldom broken except for the welcome sounds of the "Truck" Wagon Gang.

On Saying Good Bye

The morning news broke the story: two brothers had robbed a beer joint, and in attempting to escape, one had been fatally shot. The other was arrested and remained in custody in the Lee County, AL jail.

The dead man, never a candidate for the Good Citizenship Award, had been a high school mate of mine, and I volunteered to help the funeral director as I sometimes did. I was standing just inside the church door as the service was coming to a close. As the benediction was being said, my attention was diverted by the sound of a vehicle stopping out front. A well-marked deputy sheriff's vehicle was transporting the surviving brother now out on bail. As he came up the church steps, he met the people leaving the service.

The burial was in a rural cemetery some fifteen miles from the church. Pavement gave way to narrow, rutted, red clay, dirt road overarched with tree limbs and vines. One would not have been surprised if Tarzan and Cheetah were waiting around the next turn.

After the graveside service, the surviving brother asked the casket to be opened that he might say his goodbyes. He stood silently peering at his lifeless accomplice. He bent over, patted the cold hands of Charles, and said in a rather blasé manner, "Well, 'ole boy, I'll see you later." With that he turned and walked leisurely away.

Though that was a summer day some fifty-five years ago, I still get chills every time I replay that scene on the DVD of my memory.

Proceed with Caution

One funeral home serving all the small towns in a given rural county is not unusual in Alabama. One funeral home per town is more common. Two in the same town is a rarity. Two located immediately across the street from one another may be unique anywhere in the United States, regardless of population. But, that is what you will find if you take Exit 32 off I-459 and travel east on U.S. 11 into Trussville.

The funeral home on the right is surrounded by a cemetery which features an attractive, bronze-colored wrought iron fence. A natural gas pumping station abuts the property of the funeral home on the left. A silver-colored, steel, chain link fence encircles the utilities building, and a sign is attached to that section that faces the street. Its message printed in twelve-inch, bold, black letters, is easily readable by visitors in the cemetery across the road. The sign reads:

811

CALL BEFORE YOU DIG

Paradigm Shifts

The Pale Horse seldom rode alone when he galloped into my hometown. Other certainties rode on his back.

...The deceased would be guaranteed a decent funeral thanks to affordable burial insurance issued by Brown-Service Insurance Co. (The weekly premium on me was $.08).

...Whether haloed saint or one who would "bust hell wide open," the service would be held at the church out of necessity. Funeral homes were in old houses whose living room-turned chapel could hardly accommodate fifteen people. As sub-contractors to the insurance company they could afford no better.

...The family would be well-fed. Every neighbor would bring at least one casserole and a gallon of sweet tea, and the church would host the family for a meal on the day of the service.

But all of that has changed.

...Burial insurance has gone the way of the dial phone, 78 rpm record albums and analog television.

...In partnership with Brown-Service, funeral homes are now housed in attractive buildings with well-appointed chapels, ironically now less used as more and more the trend is to graveside services.

...In quest of greater profits, the funeral industry now markets an EVENT. Anything from finger foods to banquet spreads are catered and served on the premises. In chapel turned-banquet hall, one family arranged for a seated dinner, and the minister delivered the eulogy/address as the people ate their food.

Peace in The Valley

Many cemeteries now resemble residential subdivisions. One might find sections named: The Garden of Gethsemane; Garden of the Good Shepherd; Garden of the Twelve Apostles, etc. There may be sections reserved for military veterans, members of fraternal orders, etc.

Today everyone with work to do was there: the flower truck driver, directors, pallbearers, grave diggers, vault installers, and the cemetery representative.

Three guards in plain clothes were also there. Their long side arms looked as if they might have seen duty the Saturday night before on "Gun Smoke." Were they there because of vandalism? No. Were they there to investigate an accident? No. Did they have a warrant for some fugitive who might show up? No.

They had been hired to keep peace within the family that was laying a loved one to rest near, of all places, the Garden of Tranquility.

Prophecy or Curse?

As a friend of our family was having lunch at the nursing home with her father and 4 others sitting at a round table, her father, without provocation or warning, suddenly extended his arm and shook his finger in the face of the man across the table and announced in a loud voice, "You are going to heaven tonight!" Apparently not satisfied with the response of the one who received this news, the father repeated his charge, this time pointing with 2 fingers, "You are going to heaven tonight!"

The next morning his daughter, shocked and upset by her dad's bizarre behavior, went back to the nursing home to check on the well-being of the fingered man. She learned that he had been admitted to the hospital the night before. And in an even stranger development, three days later, the man died!

Piety Personified

Based on the description given me by her children, the woman I was about to bury ranked just below the blessed Virgin in the pecking order of Piety. She was a great mom, loved everybody, could out cook Paula Deen, would rank alongside Mother Teresa in helping anyone in need, worked hard, and was a woman of deep, abiding faith in and service to God.

(Since extremes always are a cover-up, I became a bit suspicious. It was then the only line I remembered from a dreadful course in Shakespeare popped into my head, "Me thinketh they protesteth too much".)

And, as if I needed further help to elevate this woman to and through the Pearly Gates, I was asked to read a poem written by a friend that further celebrated the positive, admirable characteristics of the deceased. After privately reading the poem, I asked if it would not be more appropriate and more personable for the author to read it, but that gracious offer came to naught quicker than you could say, "Somebody is pulling my leg."

This rhyme of tribute, honoring the one who earlier had been described to me as The Poster Woman for Proverbs 31, opened with the words, "Maw won't be at the bar today, she went to work for our Savior we say...?

Roller Coaster

Emotionally, ministers ride a roller coaster with more ups and downs, peaks and valleys than the Great American Scream Machine at Six Flags Over Georgia.

My first stop of the morning was the maternity ward at Brookwood Medical Center in Birmingham, AL. There I met a beaming couple who had just welcomed a new-born all adorned in pink. I offered a prayer for the safe delivery of the baby, the well-being of the mother, and for the wonderful privilege of cooperating with God in the ongoing creation of the world.

The next stop, hardly a mile away, was to visit with another couple with a new arrival. They were in a funeral home, not a hospital. Their lovely, full-term infant was still-born. There was no joy, only sorrow and heartbreak. Silence and hugs were the order of the day. Then we talked briefly about the death of the neo-natal born to David and Bathsheba. Words uttered so long ago by the king became a treasured promise. Though he could not bring back the baby, "I shall go to him...."

Remarks at Memorial Service and Marker Dedication for Christy Murphy

God has said:

"I will never leave you or forsake you" (Hebrews 13:5);

"Never despise one of these little ones. It is not your Heavenly Father's will that one of these little ones should be lost" (Matthew 18:10, 14).

"Things beyond our seeing, things beyond our hearing, things beyond our imagining, have all been prepared by God for those who love Him" (1 Corinthians 2:9).

Our meeting here today is a time of: ambivalence; mixed emotions; and contradictions of a sort. The argument can be made, however, that we shouldn't be here at all. Babies are not supposed to die; little girl toddlers are supposed to be dressed in smocked dresses, not shrouds; the average life span is 80 years, not seventeen months.

But this is a fallen world. The action on the stage does not always follow the script on the page. The Thomas family knows better than most that: the best of plans fall apart; accidents happen; bad things happen to good and innocent people.

On the other hand, it is most fitting that we are here, and are here as people of faith. Scripture instructs and the experience of the faithful confirm: God knows, cares and can make a difference. He has a long record of: working despite circumstances; bringing good out of something bad; causing light to penetrate the darkness.

Jesus became a child, birthed under less than ideal conditions; placed high value on little ones; spoke of parenthood as the most responsible job on earth. He loved children; had time for them even on his busiest days; held them in His loving embrace.

Even so, not even God always gets His druthers. Heavenly plans are not always carried out on earth. Children become ill; they suffer; they are neglected.

But, thankfully, when there are those who step out, there are others who step in. Staff, volunteers and strangers were attracted to this terminally ill little girl who gave evidence of a special bond with her twin brother; loved to be cuddled; enjoyed popcorn when her appetite was destroyed by chemo.

Visitors were touched by this child abandoned by her parents. They brought her stuffed animals, 140 in all, to lift her spirits. Upon her death her foster parents began giving them to other patients who were afraid and needed courage. The animals continue to come in under a program called Christy's Courage and are now used by police, rescue squads and ambulance crews.

And here is where you Thomas brothers enter the picture. You became aware of a need; your heart strings were touched; and you did something about it.

Not only have you set an unselfish example for others to follow, you have ministered to Christy Murphy. You have recognized her worth as a human being, given her a place, and a marked grave to keep her name alive.

You have ministered to Christ. "Whoever receives a child in my name receives me" (Matthew 18:5). "As often as you have done it unto the least of these you have done it unto me" (Matthew 25). "See that you not despise one of the least of these little ones; for I tell you in heaven their angels always behold the face of God" (Matthew 18:10).

You have ministered to your family. You have exercised responsible stewardship of resources; you have made good use of a vacant grave space. Opposite the tomb of your infant brother, there now lies beside your parents a little girl your dear mother always wanted but never had until now.

Today, we dedicate this marker, a record set in stone that Christy Murphy lived; someone took notice; someone cared.

Now we commit her spirit into the outstretched, loving arms of Christ.

"May God's gentle earth blanket her form in calm and peace as we await the final dawn."

Surprise!

Since printed obituaries often have been "sanitized," an on-call chaplain, unlike Paul Harvey, may not know "the rest of the story" until meeting with the family, if then. And then you may be as surprised at what you learn as first responders must be at what they might see at an accident scene.

The news media reported that at 2:00 A.M. the body of a man had been found in the parking lot of an apartment complex. He had been beaten, kicked and stabbed to death. A suspect had turned himself in, but three other suspects remained at large.

Police records revealed the dead man had a lengthy criminal record. His rap sheet included traffic violations, theft and resisting arrest. Only months earlier, he had been released from prison for sexually abusing a child who was under 12 years of age. Now he had been murdered.

Only after arriving at the funeral home did the connection come — the deceased and the person described in the news were one and the same!

And the surprises did not stop there.

Minutes before the service began, the mother of the deceased leaped from her seat, turned and shouted to a man in attendance, "Get out of here! I told you not to come! I don't want you in here!" And with that she chased the man from the chapel.

Could the pursued in this reality show version of the child's game "fox and hounds" be one of the suspects still on the run? Is he armed? Are the other two suspects also present? What is about to happen? Where are the police when you need them?

What do you do as officiating minister when circumstances suddenly scramble the combinations on the Scrabble board of your plans? Like a building inspector, you look for an emergency exit—whether it is so marked or not. You pray to God somebody is calling the cops. Your usual funeral homily is scrapped for a brief, and I do mean brief, evangelistic sermon based on John 3:16-18. After the service, you ask the funeral director in jest, at least partially in jest: is there a hazardous pay clause in my contract? If not, what do I need to do to get one included? Do you know where to purchase bullet-proof vests, the type big-name, political VIPS wear under their shirts?

This incident left me adopting as my own the punch line of a Holiday Inn commercial, "The best surprise is no surprise!"

Think You've Heard It All?

More than 700 people attended the funeral. Among those sending condolences were Fob James, then-governor of Alabama, Hank Williams, Jr., and Porter Waggoner. Ray Scott, founder of the Bass Angler's Sportsmen's Society, delivered the eulogy. Newspapers from five continents carried the story.

Leroy Brown was the name of the decedent. The Eufaula High School Marching Band played Jim Croce's "Big, Bad Leroy Brown" as the casket was lowered. The German-made, $4000 granite marker which bears his likeness marks the spot. The inscription reads, "Most bass are just fish, but Leroy Brown was special."

Leroy was caught by world-renowned fisherman, Tom Mann, in 1973. He ruled eight years in a 40-foot long aquarium at Tom Mann's Fish World in Eufaula, Alabama.

He died in 1981 and was buried with honors befitting "the world's most famous fish".

To Err Is Human

To personalize the funeral of a woman he did not know, the minister I had engaged asked the son for information about his deceased mother. The data he received was as brief as a telegram. The son's response was, you are the professional; handle it like you wish.

Needing to say something but with little something to say, the minister spoke mostly in generalities. Seeking to be kind, complimentary and affirming, he closed his remarks with the reading of Proverbs 31:10-31. This passage extols the virtue, industry and conscientiousness of the model woman-wife-mother. (It was penned by Solomon whose considerable experience in the field of marriage made him one who ought to know.)

Following the service, the son approached the minister in a somewhat sheepish manner. "I guess I should have told you, but I didn't. I kinda let you hang out to dry. It's all my fault. But everybody here knows my mother was a (substitute a homophone for witch.)"

The director in charge and I had overseen the placing of the casket on the lowering device and the seating of the family. It was time to begin.

Following the reading of Scripture and prayer the minister explained, "We will now have two songs. One is the favorite "How Great Thou Art." I am not familiar with the other one but based on what I have been told of this lady's reputation as a Christian, I'm sure it is also a good hymn of the church." Hardly!

"Ah! Sweet Mystery of Life" is from the 1935 movie version of "Naughty Marietta." Set in New Orleans, it is the story of Captain Richard Warrington's' commission to capture a notorious pirate, a quest sometimes helped and sometimes impeded by the high-spirited runaway, Countess Marietta.

But there was precedent. Jeanette McDonald was to sing that song at the funeral of actress Jean Harlow. She became so overcome with grief as to be unable to finish the song. Nelson Eddy immediately stepped in, put his arms around her shoulder and finished the assignment.

Even so, "Ah! Sweet Mystery of Life" is yet to appear in my hymnal. And the minister continues to wipe egg residue from his face.

The Death of a President

Tired from a grueling week of rehearsals, busy preparing for the next night's televised final of the Miss Alabama Pageant on which there was riding thousands of dollars in scholarships and perhaps career possibilities, what the 48 contestants wanted least of all was an impromptu visit to a funeral home, of all places.

Former President Ronald Reagan had died the day before (June 5, 2004). The mortuary moguls of the nationwide chain handling the funeral arrangements had mandated register books and that they be placed in all their installations coast to coast to give red-blooded Americans the opportunity to express their patriotism and honor an esteemed leader. (No word was mentioned this was a great opportunity for free, national corporate advertising neatly wrapped in red, white and blue.)

Since the pageant did have patriotic overtones—the winner would compete in the Miss America contest—and since the death of our 40th president was of historic note, pageant leadership decided a trip to sign the register book would be worthwhile.

Two chartered motor coaches brought the lovelies from the Samford University campus to a local funeral home. Not even their considerable beauty could camouflage their lack of interest in being there. After all, this man left office when they were only in first and second grade. Their interest was not ancient history but concentrating on the four components on which they would be judged (interviews, talent, swim suit, evening gown).

And if this were not enough, they would have to stand outside for a memorial service, their high heels leaving small pock marks in the parking lot's hot asphalt. Moreover, the speaker would not be a Brad Pitt type, but an old, wrinkled, worn out preacher.

Fortunately for me, their previous stop -had NOT been the State Farmers' Market where they might have bought tomatoes.

The Body: Whole or Parts

The following emerged when I was asked to do the research by a terminally ill man and a group of his friends.

You can legally sell blood or plasma, but the Uniform Anatomical Donor Act (1984), made it illegal to sell or buy body parts though there are more than 140,000 names on a waiting list for transplantable organs with one new name added every 11 minutes. Despite the fact one donor can save up to 8 lives, the shortage of available parts results in 20 deaths per day in the United States (U.S. Department of Health and Human Services, March 2011).

When it comes to whole body donation, the situation is not unlike buying season tickets to the big-time college football games; you must pay a premium to purchase. Locally, to unselfishly donate your body for scientific research and medical education, a person must pay $750 for the privilege of becoming a cadaver! Even then, it is not tax deductible... ...and there are restrictions.

When discussing the 200 pound-or-less body weight-limit with the group, a man who would tip the scales at twice that smiled and said, "Well, I guess I could donate an arm."

The Amputee

I introduced myself to the wife who, except for the obvious presence of her dear friend, Jack Daniels, sat alone in the funeral home foyer. As was my custom, I explained my usual approach which causes most—when they find out the service will not be long, a tear-jerker or end with an altar call—to express a W-H-E-W that simulates the tire on a giant tractor-trailer going flat. Not this woman. Her dead-pan silence was finally broken when she explained her husband's amputation in layman's terms. "They chopped his leg off."

I saw a note posted for the staff, "They want his cowboy boot(s) back," and it also stated the family would furnish a CD of the song they wanted played.

Suffering from less than information overload, I took my chair in the chapel. My remarks would follow the playing of the song. It was Joe Diffie's, "Prop Me Up by the Juke Box If I Die."

That request was honored, but I thought I might need the help of the widow's friend, Jack Daniels, to regain my composure. And if that were not enough, the director suddenly developed a "limp" as we moved from the hearse to the gravesite.

The Exorcism

As though they were Ringling Brothers, Barnum and Bailey Circus elephants walking single file from their railroad cars to the big top to perform, five sleek limousines followed the black hearse, its polished color glistening in the sun like the spit-shined boots of a U.S. Marine. The escort-led entourage came to a stop on the narrow cemetery lane that offered the closest street access to the grave. The mourners and friends quietly stood beside their fancy means of transport as the white-gloved pall bearers executed their solemn duty.

Decorum had gone well until a sudden gust of wind, as though responding to some mysterious cue, blew the beautiful flowers from atop the casket to the ground. From the dismayed crowd there came a cry of panic, "What was that?" That was followed by an anonymous, stentorian declaration, "The Devil!" to which the questioner exclaimed in a voice loud enough to wake the dead, "Come out of there, Sapsucker!"

No doubt ministerial-led pandemonium would have resulted had the corpse come back to life as did Lazarus in ancient Bethany. Instead, a lesser miracle occurred. The exorcism, more akin to the dispatch of swine at Gadara, worked!

With that, a sense of jittery calm was restored as quickly as the disquieting wind had come. The committal service continued in an orderly but somewhat accelerated manner but befitting the proper disposition of the beloved dead. After the benediction, neither the crowd nor clergyman lingered, and some were seen looking over their shoulder as they beat a hasty retreat to their cars.

Would you venture a guess as to whose vehicle was the first through the exit gate?

Equal Representation

If the cherished American institution of free enterprise is being threatened as some believe, word has not yet reached the funeral and funeral related business. Instead of simply whining about the negative toll cremation has taken on their bottom line, ingenuity has shifted into high gear. Whereas the disposition of cremains—the sugarcoated term for ashes—largely was limited to urns on a shelf, scattering or dumping in the ocean, those days are as dated as the steam locomotive, the six-ounce bottled Coke and the wing-tipped shoes.

There now are as many options as a smorgasbord at an all-you-can-eat, roadside hash house whose grease-laden, calorie-loaded offerings will give you indigestion so badly you wish you were dead.

Sea burial has been updated too. Some urns now are made of biodegradable sea salt; others of heavier material sink and become a man-made reef.

One company is taking reservation for its space launch with a payload of cremains for those who want to get a jumpstart on their trip to heaven.

Scientists are now doing with cremains what they had learned to do with tequila, turn them into diamonds for rings, pendants, bracelets and necklaces—giving new meaning to an old saying, "they will wear on you."

Not to be outdone, two entrepreneurial Alabama game wardens have organized company aimed (no pun intended) at the outdoors type. Furnish them with a pound of cremains and they will pack them into the payload of 250 shotgun shells. According to their web page, they also offer a "mantel-worthy" wooden storage box for the shells with the name of the deceased engraved.

In a cleverly written article, Mike Bolton, hunting/fishing columnist for the local newspaper, turned advocate for equal rights and equal representation: "After so many shotgun weddings in Alabama, it's about time somebody came up with a shotgun funeral" (The Birmingham News, July 3, 2011).

The New Columbarium

Cremation is the fastest growing segment in the funeral industry. According to the National Funeral Directors' Association, cremations in Alabama are projected to rise from the current 9.73 to 24.25% by the year 2025. Nationally, the projected figure moves upward from 24.1% to 58.25%.

Because of this rapidly growing popularity, for many churches—some who got out of the cemetery business because of its attendant headaches, are now constructing columbaria. A columbarium, from a Latin root meaning dove resting place, is "a place for the respectful and usually public storage of cinerary urns (those containing cremated human remains) in niches or cubicles. The columbarium may be free standing or a part of another building."

One suburban church, widely known for the sale of its cooked-on-the-premises barbecue which benefits the Building Fund, recently decided to build a columbarium. Their pre-construction promotional brochure identified the placement of the structure as being on the church property "near the barbecue pit".

A week later, I saw the minister of the church— a longtime friend and Phi Beta Kappa graduate—and congratulated him on the new endeavor. We talked about potential problems associated with the project, and then I said, "Based on the advertised location of the columbarium on the church grounds, transportation of cremains should not be an issue."

Grinning, but embarrassed by the failure of some proof-reader, his face turned as red as any flame ever generated in a cremation chamber.

The Will of God

What a difference a day makes!

Having kissed his wife good-bye, the man left for another day at the office. He enjoyed lunch with two friends, me among them. When the work was done, he returned home only to find his wife dead in the floor! She apparently had suffered a heart attack early that morning while making up the bed.

As one of the first on the scene, I found a distraught, restless man pacing the floor and asking over and again the usual tormenting questions: "Why? Why her? What if I had not gone to work? What if I had called her?" I put my arm around his shoulders and suggested he scream, cuss, knock a hole in the wall, do whatever he needed to do to release some of the emotional pressure.

In a follow-up visit he asked if I remembered what I had told him. Then he said, "If you had told me, this is the will of God, I think I would have punched you out."

At another time and in a different place, a set of parents never forgave me for not saying their teenager's death was the will of God. In fact, they joined another church because of that. In their hurt and pain, they found it easier to accept that death as part of a divine plan rather than to come to grips with the truth of the police report. The young man was responsible for his own demise as well as that of two companions. Possessed with a sense of invincibility, as young (and old) men so often are, and driving while impaired, they turned a high-powered automobile into a toy which proved to be no match in a showdown with a big-rig, tractor trailer.

There are certain risks that go with being human. Who is exempt from the limitations that are part and parcel of our finiteness when, for whatever reason, our bodies wear out or are subjected to forces greater than our ability to survive?

The God revealed in Jesus Christ is not a serial killer, a crime for which a person would be sentenced to capital punishment, whose capricious acts we are to accept as beneficent. A God like that is more demonic than divine. Rather, the Scripture teaches God receives the faithful into his nearer presence once *death* has taken them.

Taps: An Encore

At the funerals of many honorably discharged veterans the family will request an honor guard of three uniformed personnel from the veteran's branch of service—two to fold the flag and one to play "Taps".

To compensate for the lack of capable or available buglers, the instruments are equipped with tape players, operated by on/off switches that play the haunting sound of our national song of remembrance.

At the appointed time, the soldier lifted the instrument to his lips, holding it there until the somber notes were over. He then slowly lowered the horn and at that point, the bugler became the bungler. In returning the bugle to its case, he accidentally tripped the on switch, and the family was treated to a "Taps" encore.

The WORD

Often the church in the South has been called the most segregated institution in the country, and not without some merit. However, a strong case can be made that designation more aptly describes the funeral industry of the region. But as Bob Dylan's song says, "The Times They are a-Changin".

I have conducted six funerals for African American families. They all have been for females, and they range in age from stillborns to centenarians. The most recent was for a ninety-eight-year-old whose family came over from Atlanta to make arrangements.

Deacon Bogart, the son-in-law, told the funeral home manager everything was in place but one; they needed a preacher. The manager asked, "Does it matter if the minister is not African American? The reason I ask is I don't have any contacts among the black clergy. I know I can enlist a white." The deacon thought for a moment and then responded, "The Word is the Word."

On my way to the service I recalled the words of Halford Luccock, a prominent Methodist minister of yesteryear and professor of homiletics at Yale Divinity School. In his book on funerals he contended the greatest improvement ministers could make in delivering funeral orations would be in the inclusion of more Scripture reading.

Deacon Bogart was on to something. The Word is the Word. It speaks as no other to the deepest needs of all people be they of any race or region, illiterate or erudite rabble or refined, men of poverty or men of plenty. The Word is the Word.

The Patriot in Short Pants

Our family were still newcomers to Lanett when World Blood Bath II ended in 1945. The funeral for the first, local, fallen hero was the talk of the town.

On the morning of that service I walked to the cemetery, only a block from our house. A crew of four city workers were digging the grave by hand. As I watched I wondered if there was some way I could honor the young man who died in defense of freedom, my freedom. With that, I hesitatingly asked one of the workers if I could help. Rather than dismiss my offer by saying, "No, you are too small, we'll handle it," he smiled and handed me his shovel. I was no match for the hard, dry clay, and I gave it my best effort. But I felt I had had a part.

During the war I proudly had saved quarters to buy bonds—it took seventy-five quarters to reach the $18.75 price of one that was worth $25.00 at maturity. And to this day I am grateful to that man that allowed a ten-year-old kid in short pants to make a small, patriotic contribution in peace just as he had done before the guns were silenced.

Unwanted Visitors

"Dear Abby: Are there any rules of etiquette involving unwanted guests at funerals?" wrote a woman concerned about the possibility of undesirables at her service. And her husband wanted to know how in the world you would keep them away.

Abby cleverly suggested two ways. "Outlive your enemies," but if you predecease them, make sure the public knows this is an "invitation only event" by stating such in the obituary.

Experience has taught me a third and fourth option if the others do not work.

The wife of the deceased, his second, was adamant that she did not want the former spouse and her husband's children present at the chapel. This tall, well-dressed woman wearing a black hat that would have turned Greta Garbo green with envy had several one-on-one private conversations with the director during the visitation. Soon I would know why.

Suddenly the director greeting guests at the door said, "Uh oh". The first wife and her brood had just pulled into the parking lot at the funeral home. He quickly locked the door, shouted to the receptionist, "Call the cops!" and he headed down the hall to secure a second door with me wondering what was going on, trailing close behind.

The unwanted, discovering the doors locked, quietly returned to their car and left.

If you don't outlive your enemies and if the undesirables don't get the message, make sure the funeral home doors have strong locks. And if this fails, get a restraining order from the courts and let the cops serve as doormen.

Unwanted Still Born

Because the parents were illegally in the United States, burying the still born Guatemalan fell on the responsibility of the father's brother. (The father had dropped out of sight immediately.) On short notice, I was called to conduct the Friday afternoon graveside service. Through Social Services of Children's' Hospital, generous people had donated lots in several cemeteries for such purposes.

I arrived that blistering hot day, Spanish New Testament in hand, but no grave had been dug. No one apparently had notified the cemetery, and it would be Monday before the service could be scheduled.

Fortunately, I was able to call a man fluent in Spanish, and in a thirty-minute cell phone tag match between him and the director, and between him and the uncle, everyone understood the predicament as well as the new plan.

Standing there I thought if such were happening to me in a country not my own, and unable to communicate in that country's language, I would have suspected that someone was messing with me. Not that uncle. Though disappointed, he was gracious and said he understood how mistakes happen.

By Monday I was able to enlist an interpreter and the service went smoothly.

It is Well with My Soul

At the time of the death of my dear mother-in-law, and unknown to the family, the funeral home-cemetery where she had made pre-arrangements was, itself, on life-support. A cash-strapped, bureaucratic-laden, state agency had been called in as the specialist to slow the death rattle of a mismanaged business owned by folk who seemed to be as adept at milking profits as my in-law's dairyman neighbor was at milking his fine herd of Holsteins. The staff had been down-sized to a receptionist and an as-needed grave digger. All other services had been outsourced to entities and individuals who worked as free-lancing, independent contractors. Her body was prepared by an out-of-town embalmer, her casket expressed-shipped across Alabama from Livingston, on the Mississippi line, to Lanett, on the Georgia line. A funeral director from LaGrange, Georgia was to work the service. He was a man the receptionist didn't know but was told he would be there, but she had her doubts. The logistics chart looked like a Rube Goldberg contraption. Lack of communication would have rivaled that of FEMA in the wake of Hurricane Katrina. Anxiety would have registered on the Richter Scale. But in retrospect it was all biblical: "The right hand did not know what the left hand was doing."

The receptionist, who would put in a ten-hour day, was a basket case. Tearfully she shared her chief concern, whether the funeral director would come as she had been told, a concern exacerbated by Alabama law requiring the presence of a licensed director. I explained that I was state-licensed. I would direct it, and the funeral would legally proceed as planned even if he were a no-show. Her sigh of relief sounded like air escaping from a punctured tire on an eighteen-wheeler.

For my own peace of mind, I checked out the hearse which had to be operational no matter what. It had not been cranked in weeks, and I was sure the battery was a dead as any corpse it ever had transported. The sound of that engine turning over was as sweet as an angel's song. Next, a brother-in-law and I attacked the knee-high grass in front of the building with a weed-eater. Having neither the time nor a baler, we blew our harvest into a near-by ditch. Then we mowed the area around the grave site. But preparation work still was not complete. Learning there was neither flower truck nor driver, we utilized his vehicle and the receptionist's van to transport the many beautiful wreaths. As on-the-job-trained florists, we also arranged them in the church and at the grave.

Thankfully, the funeral went without a hitch. The weather was ideal, the director showed up, the hearse cranked, the flowers were beautiful, and the ministers did an outstanding job.

Only a handful of people were aware of the logistically-induced angst. By swift action, elbow grease and a special measure of the grace of God, what could have been an ugly, embarrassing episode, coming at the worst possible time, was avoided.

Did You Ever Think When the Hearse Went By...?

An article in *The Daily Undertaker* (August 30, 2000) speaks of a funeral possession as "a respectful and ceremonious transport of a person to their final place of rest which allows the town to see that expression of love and respect." It is a way of saying:

- this day is unlike other days;
- this person was important to us;
- this journey is not like other journeys;
- a special vehicle is used to transport our love one to a special place of honor and memory.
- That was then, this now:
- urban streets bustle with traffic;
- there are appointments to make and places to be.
- processions are an interruption and often engender road rage.

In short, funeral processions are on the endangered species list. Many funeral homes are adjacent to cemeteries and don't require a procession. With cremations growing in popularity, many are never buried. Yet, safety is a growing concern.

Sometimes the danger is from without. In one procession I was a part of we were moving on a four-lane thoroughfare with police escorts. The lead escort, for no apparent reason, decided to stop traffic in all directions. Two oncoming cars quickly pulled to the side and stopped. When the driver of the third car, apparently distracted, looked up and saw tail lights, rather than rear end car two, he pulled hard to the right and jumped the curb. The car climbed a giant oak, fell on its top, and bounced two times in the street. The driver was unhurt, but the accident would have been preventable but for an officer's Barney Fyffe complex.

Sometimes the danger is from within. A lady in the procession decided to break rank. Apparently never looking in the mirror, she pulled out to the left and struck and killed one of the escorts on his way to block traffic at the upcoming intersection.

These dangers have led many communities to outlaw processions.

The death of the funeral cortege with all its symbolism may be distasteful to some and seen as disrespectful to many, but it now joins the ever-widening and growing endangered species list attributed to urbanization.

Perhaps our fast-paced, modern culture could benefit from the words of British statesman, Sir William Gladstone (1809-98): "Show me the way a nation cares for its dead, and I will measure with mathematical exactness the tender mercies of its people, their respect for the laws of the land and their loyalty to high ideals."

We Preach Our Own Funeral

Each of us preaches our own funeral. It is a task we do every day. Its content is determined by our relationship to God in Christ, the uses to which we put our time, talent and influence; the causes we serve and the investments we make with our love. To wit:

Dolores Aguilar
1929 - Aug. 7, 2008

Dolores Aguilar, born in 1929 in New Mexico, left us on August 7, 2008. She will be met in the afterlife by her husband, Raymond, her son, Paul Jr., and daughter, Ruby. She is survived by her daughters Marietta, Mitzi, Stella, Beatrice, Virginia and Ramona, and son Billy; grandchildren, Donnelle, Joe, Mitzie, Maria, Mario, Marty, Tynette, Tania, Leta, Alexandria, Tommy, Billy, Mathew, Raymond, Kenny, Javier, Lisa, Ashlie and Michael; great-grandchildren, Brendan, Joseph, Karissa, Jacob, Delaney, Shawn, Cienna, Bailey, Christian, Andrea Jr., Andrea, Keith, Saeed, Nujaymah, Salma, Merissa, Emily, Jayci, Isabella, Samantha and Emily. I apologize if I missed anyone.

Dolores had no hobbies, made no contribution to society and rarely shared a kind word or deed in her life. I speak for the majority of her family when I say her presence will not be missed by many, very few tears will be shed and there will be no lamenting over her passing.

Her family will remember Dolores and amongst ourselves we will remember her in our own way, which were mostly, sad and troubling times through the years. We may have some fond memories of her and perhaps we will think of those times too. But I truly believe at the end of the day ALL of us will only miss what we never had, a good and kind mother, grandmother and great-grandmother. I hope she is finally at peace with herself. As for the rest of us left behind, I hope this is the beginning of a time of healing and learning to be a family again.

There will be no service, no prayers and no closure for the family she spent a lifetime tearing apart. We cannot come together in the end to see to it that her grandchildren and great-grandchildren can say their goodbyes. So, I say to her for all of us, GOOD BYE, MOM.

Weighty Matters

Six is the usual number of pallbearers, but the director advised we might wish we had 8 in this case. Was he for real or joking?

To satisfy my curiosity, immediately upon arriving at the funeral home, I made my way down the hall to get a view of the one lying supine in the parlor. He wasn't joking! That lady was l-a-r-g-e. The other 5 bearers greeted the news with groans.

Preparing to move to the cemetery, the 6 of us lined up at the door to carry the casket to the hearse. The daughter, preceding the casket, stopped and graciously expressed her gratitude for our help. Our smiles were cut short by her next words, "Hope no one gets hurt."

The grave was at least 40 yards off the road and up a slight slope, a perfect profile for 6 simultaneous hernias! Absent heavy-lifting equipment from Crane Works, the cemetery graciously consented for the hearse to pull up to the grave.

Who Will Guard the Guard?

Barney Fife lives! Sometimes he is the playground bully; sometimes the Pink Lady behind the hospital information desk; sometimes the deacon in a church; and most definitely in certain members of law enforcement who have both badge and bullet.

Our procession, led by 3 escorts, pulled on to a major, 4 lane thoroughfare. Traffic was light, and we were traveling in the curb-side lane. Apparently fueled by a rush of macho mania and a surge to show who was boss, the lead escort, straddling the center line, decided to stop traffic in 2 oncoming lanes.

Two oncoming vehicles quickly slowed, pulled to the side and came to a stop. The driver of the vehicle following them, either on the phone or perhaps texting, sees brake lights and he panics. He slammed on brakes, cut sharply to the right, jumped the curb, and like a squirrel, the car began climbing a giant water oak tree. It then fell upside down in the street. The driver escaped through a window and began beating the car with his fists. The vehicle had been punished enough and was now absorbing blows meant for a cop who richly deserved them.

Where There Is A Will

A guy whose black dress shirt was highlighted by a light-colored sport coat and bright tie arrogantly paced the floor of the funeral home foyer as though he were a caged lion in a zoo. He gave the impression he could strut while sitting. After a few minutes his restlessness became contagious. I got it! What was going on? Who was this guy? Heavy set and well built, was he Vito the Enforcer from the Mafia? Or was he Bruno the Bouncer from the Platinum Club?

When the director announced the family would meet in the parlor, Mr. Big Ike took charge. As lawyer for the deceased he would read the last will and testament before the group would leave for the graveside service. And with that he closed the parlor door.

Some minutes later the door opened. As the people exited for the short ride to the cemetery—just outside the back door of the building—the staff began removing flowers, placed the casket in the hearse and the procession began.

As we gathered under the tent an interesting development took place. Of the twenty or so who had gathered in the parlor, only 10 were able to make their way to the cemetery!

It gave me new interpretive insight into the old saying, "Where there is a will there is a way."

Obits

The obit for Antonia W. Larroux, a Huntsville, AL woman, was picked up by the New York Times because her daughter discovered they would run it online for free. The pastor who conducted the funeral for this loyal customer of Waffle House was referred to as a "questionable choice for any spiritual event," but there was only one member who objected, and that was because, "every time Toni heard Curt preach she prayed for Jesus to return at that very moment." Two children resulted from her marriage, but "due to multiple, anonymous Mother's Day cards, the children suspect there were other siblings but that has never been verified." She considered Aaron Burrell—"who had the ability with family pets to usher them toward heaven at an unrivaled pace"—to be a "distant grandson, but not distant enough."

"Anyone wearing black will not be admitted to the memorial."

"...and by his nieces and nephews who affectingly called his 'Uncle Jack.'"

"She will be greatly missed by those closest to her. 'I see the moon and the moon sees me. God bless the moon and God bless me.'"

"She was lovingly known by many others in addition to her? grands? and as? Nanny? a role she played beautifully."

"He was a member of Christ Chapel and an avid Alabama Football Van."

"Fred's readings soured from prior annual average of one hundred books to one hundred and fifty books."

"He is survived by his husband, Walter."

"GARRISON, MARGARET, Baton Rogue, LA."

Among the survivors ...brother, "Gun Control;" and trusted "Detroit Alley Dog." Goat a 35-year devil's disciple dedicated his life to his brothers and love of the Club."

"In lieu of flowers, the family respectfully asked that donations be sent to the American Cancer Society or to the campaign of whoever is running against President Barak Obama in 2012.

"In case of inclement weather, the service will be held at the Southside Club. (Photo ID will be required for entry.)

"She will be laid to rest by her husband at Bethel Memorial Cemetery."

More Obits

"Upon the death of her mother at age ten, her father reared his large family alone."

"He excepted Christ at an early age."

"You and Papa are together again, and you couldn't take anything with you to hit (your welcome Papa)-We love you and miss you."

"Her chopped liver was a highly anticipated event."

"Until his last moments, he anxiously looked forward to the day the Lord would welcome him into heaven."

"She is preceded in death by her son Randy (deceased)."

About the mother of eight: "She spent her lifetime torturing in every way possible. While she neglected and abused her small children, she refused to allow anyone else to care or show compassion toward them. ...Everyone she met... was tortured by her cruelty and exposure to violence, criminal activity, vulgarity and hated of the gentle or kind human spirit.

"On behalf of her children whom she abusively exposed to her evil and violent life, we celebrate her passing from this earth and hope she lives in the afterlife reliving each gesture of violence, cruelty and shame she delivered on her children. Her surviving children will now live with the peace of knowing their nightmare finally has some form of closure.

"Our greatest wish now is to stimulate a national movement that mandates a purposeful and dedicated war against child abuse in the United States of America."

". . . was a member of the Merry Diggers Garden Club and was an honorary life member of the Alabama Funeral directors Association."

"She was born unexpectedly...in her own grandparents' bed—her mother...had been canning fruit and mistook the early labor pains for having eaten too many peaches."

"He is survived by his uncle...a left-handed pitcher for the Boston Red Socks in the 1930's."

"He planted hundreds of trees in his lifetime, made furniture, drank tea and smoked the hookah pipe.... May he rest in peace."

"He worked at Lloyd Noland Hospital before it closed as an accountant."

Last of Last Words

Having described the woman's favorite foods, "OH. .and anyone who knew her knew never to go head to head with her in a burping contest."

"He and Kay married during college and later had children.

"He married his wife in 1950 and was able to celebrate 33 years of marriage at the time of her death."

"...a well-known Baptist Minister who pastured numerous churches."

"Burial in George Washing Carver Cemetery."

"She always ordered fried chicken, her father's favorite Southern dish."

"He was known for his famous saying, I'm still pretty."

Among his accomplishments, "raising two sons who have thus far avoided criminal records."

"He met what seems like an untimely death in a canoeing accident."

"Putting his mistakes and failings aside he was a good man."

"She fell off the bleachers and Glenn caught her and didn't let her go for 61 years."

After listing and naming three sons and five daughters, survivors also include "His special children (you know who you are)."

"...never married but survived by more friends, nieces and nephews than could fit in an entire newspaper."

Describing a man's birth date, he "began the day before the year after Pearl Harbor."

Dear Abby: My mother is in her mid-90's and in good health. She has no intention of dying soon, but she asked me an interesting question. She has mileage points with a major airline and was wondering if she can use them for the "final trip" back to her home state for burial when the time comes. Do you know the answer?

Dear One-way: ...I contacted a spokesman for a major airline who responded that his company does not accept mileage points as a type of payment for any type of "shipment." For her last flight, your mother would no longer be considered a passenger; she would be cargo, which is why her points won't fly.

A Miracle

Dawn Farnsworth of Brownsville, TN waited in vain day after day for the return of the man who stood her up after promising to marry her. She would walk slowly to the bus station, bag in hand, hoping for his return and growing more mentally ill every day. She would end up institutionalized where she died.

This real-life story supposedly is the inspiration behind Alex Harvey's composition, "Delta Dawn," made popular by Tanya Tucker (top 10 finish in 1972) and Helen Ready (No. 1 in 1973).

With no knowledge of that background and context—not that it would have mattered—that was the song the two sisters chose for their mother's funeral. In reality, they only cared about the last 8 words in the chorus, "to take you to that mansion in the sky." Their apparent reason was twofold; that was a song "Mama used to sing," and it embodied their hopes for Mama's final resting place.

The staff musician almost went into shock when handed the lyrics. Plus, she would have to sing it a cappella. I, seeking to relieve her angst through comic relief, whispered to her, "Did you know there is a representative here from the County Music Association, and this is your audition?" That only compounded her fear for she thought I was serious. She managed to struggle through. But noticeably there was considerably less tremolo in her voice than tremor in her hands and knees.

Why this family insisted on having a minister remains as much a mystery as the location of Jimmy Hoffa's body. Had they been asked, what is your church preference? No one would have been surprised if their answer had been, "red brick." Yet they allowed me to observe a miracle... Of a sort.

Apparently through special knowledge divinely revealed only to them, the words of a country-western song were canonized as Scripture. And as water turned into wine at Cana, they miraculously transformed the broken pledge of Harvey's "mysterious, dark-haired man," a "man of low degree," into a promise from the lips of Jesus fulfilled in their midst that day.

The truth of an adage that sprung full-grown from the womb of "the end justifies the means," was again demonstrated, "He who has a goal in mind makes all things work."

A Sibling Relationship as Cold as the Corpse

On the coolest morning of the year, neighbors found a nude, dead man on the back porch of his rural house. When authorities notified his sister, the next of kin, she responded with a statement that revealed a sibling relationship icier than the weather. "Do what you want to with him. Put him in a plastic bag and do away with him for all I care." Later she agreed to a graveside service with visitation beforehand.

When I met the sister in the parlor, her first words to me were, "Man, it is c-o-l-d outside. I got some whiskey in the car if you want a stiff belt." Being a life—long teetotaler, not wishing to invite the ire of my fellow Baptists who, unlike the Methodists, will not speak to each other in the liquor store) and fearing censorship by the ghost of the Women's Temperance Union, I graciously declined.

"I want it short," she said. I suggested the reading of Psalm 23, without which I didn't know you could conduct a funeral, and a brief passage from John 14. With the authority of a boot camp drill sergeant at Quantico Marine base, she barked, "I said short!"

At 1:30 pm, she said to the director, "Let's go." He explained there still was a half-hour left for visitation. "Look, I'm ready to go. I told folks about the visitation, and it looks like no one is coming. I am ready to go." With that she, husband and a friend, the only three in attendance, headed for their car.

At the grave, I thought of a paraphrased version of an adage, "hell hath no fury like a woman half-smashed," and not wishing to invoke the wrath of such a person, I repeated the Lord's Prayer, and that was it.

Ten minutes before the service was to begin, I was leaving the cemetery cold and sober on my way to the warmth of home and family.

Adios

I had a long-time friendship with the deceased who worked at a hardware store that I visited frequently. He was not active in any church, so I was not surprised when the call came to conduct the service.

During WW Il he had served in the Merchant Marine where he stayed in and around many of the ports of Mexico. There he had learned some pidgin Spanish which served him well with an increase in the number of Mexican customers. He had developed an affinity for Latin culture, and he had made many Latino friends locally.

Upon entering the funeral home, I could hear music from the chapel with a distinctive south-of-the-border sound. Inside there was a three-member mariachi band in full regalia. The only tune I recognized was their final one, one they had customized for the occasion. They turned from the folk in the chapel, faced the casket and sang, "Vaya con Dios, amigo. Vaya con Dios, my friend," (Go with God, amigo. Go with God my friend). Such may have been inappropriate for some folk, but it was most fitting for this man.

The band made its way to the cemetery, some fifteen miles away. They were still playing and singing as I started for home—craving a taco.

An Overstated Demise

"Brother, Jim" the familiar voice said laughingly on the phone, "we are going to need your help. And I am going to tell you exactly what the family said to me."

The family told him their mother died ten years ago. Now it was their dad, and they would be coming in from out of state.

"We would like to have the same preacher that did Mother's, but we are not sure if he is even still around. He was getting way along in years back then." "Sure, Scott," I said in jest, "I will be happy to help you locate him if I can."

As though he were the prophet Nathan addressing David (2 Samuel 12), he quickly retorted, "You are the man!"

That was three years ago. Old Methuselah is still upright, getting about, cashing my Social Security checks and occasionally conducting funerals for folk for whom I have a mad on.

A Kaleidoscope of Death

Three first-time experiences awaited me while on a preaching mission in south Alabama, each associated with death in one way or the other.

(1) The hospitable family that hosted me lived half way between the cemetery and the church. This was my first week in "purgatory".

(2) For recreation, I was treated to a demonstration of domesticated rabbits being killed for market. Like garments being dried on an exterior, linear, solar —powered clothes dryer, 20 rabbits in a row were attached by their hind legs to a clothes line. The vendor moved from one bunny to another, then wrapped his hand around the neck of each cottontail and broke its neck with a downward jerk. This was the first time, and pray God, the last for me to witness.

(3) On the third day, I traveled to a near-by town to assist with the funeral of a friend's mother. The host pastor, in his finest stentorian, Sunday voice, closed the service with these words, "By the authority invested in me as the pastor of the First Baptist Church of Hartford, I now transfer the name of Bessie Jones from the church roll to the Lamb's Book of Life." I immediately tried to kiss his ring. This was my first audience with a pope.

B as In Bitter Cold and Brevity

We left the funeral just after eight for the fifty-mile trip to the north. The day was damp and gloomy. The high would be 41 degrees. The cold still penetrated despite long-handles, overcoat, scarf and ear muffs.

Among those gathered at the grave site was the 90-year-old sister of the deceased. Brought by relatives to the cemetery, neither she nor her light sweater were a match for the weather. She, however, was insisting the casket be opened. The director called me aside and asked what I thought we should do. My cynical remark, born partly out of concern for this lady's need to be out of the weather as soon as possible as well as of my own misery, I replied, "Make them aware of the possibility of a frost-bitten corpse and don't forget the directions to this place. That poor surviving sister will be dead of pneumonia within a week and we will be back."

The casket was opened, and the mourners passed by, shaking from the cold like aspen trees in the wind, and I conducted the service. The director swears to this day I spoke for only 3 minutes, and not the first person complained.

He and I were friends before, now we are friends for life.

Bargain Basement Burials

Jessica Mitford, in her book *The American Way of Death* (1967), excoriated the funeral industry as too institutionalized and far too expensive. She further protested these perceived excesses and tried to prove her allegations by preplanning her own no-frills arrangements which would cost a grand total of only $533.31, only about $83 more than a blanket of flowers for the casket costs these days.

Passers-by must have wondered what was taking place in that open field. A small group of people were standing around a six-inch hole in the earth's surface as if it were February 2, Groundhog Day, awaiting the annual emergence of Punxsutawney Phil. For sure there was nothing to suggest a funeral—no backhoe, no tent, no chairs, no lowering device, no flower stands, no hearse, no men in dark suits, no latest fashions in women's wear.

Taking his cue from his timepiece, the son, who had excavated the opening with hole-diggers "in the presence of God and these witnesses," opened the trunk of his vehicle and retrieved his father's cremains, one of our Mary Poppins like sugar-coated euphemisms that is supposed to make the medicine of a person's demise more palatable to mourners. The ashes were contained in an eighteen- inch long by four-inch piece of PVC pipe capped on either end and securely held in place by an epoxy glue. Handwritten with a Sharpie permanent marker were the man's full name, date of birth and date of death. Really all that is necessary since death is the great equalizer.

Certain everyone was present who was supposed to be, the son nodded for me to begin. Earlier he had told me in a rather firm tone, "Make it simple." In perfect keeping with the tenor of the occasion and his drill sergeant-like command, I did. And it would take only a shovel full of dirt to fill the grave.

Somewhere in the Great Beyond, Jessica Mitford was smiling.

B.J.

B.J. and I were the same age. We had grown up together. She and her family always had lived near the state line (AL-GA) and the poverty line. Both parents were now dead. Her only sibling, a sister, burned to death in a mobile home, along with her sister's handicapped son, who started the fire while playing with matches.

B.J. lived in one side of a sub-standard, rented duplex. How her car continued to run remained a mystery to local mechanics.

She had worked forty years for minimum wage at a convenience store, almost exclusively on the 7-11 or 11-7 shifts. A kind, humble, unassuming person, she greeted every customer, friend or stranger, with "Love 'Ya darling." Policemen from two municipalities and the county often stopped in for coffee, breaking the late-night monotony for her and themselves.

As she left work one night, little did she realize she was being followed by three thugs looking for drug money. They waited until she had gone inside and then knocked on her door. When she opened the door, they cut her body in two with blasts from a shotgun. This heinous act aroused the citizenry. Why B.J. of all people? She could not have had $10.00 to her name. And she would have given them or anyone else her last dime if only they had asked. Senseless, cruel, and cold-blooded! Public outrage caused the local radio station to suspend their country-western music to become talk radio. That outlet for venting frustration plus the quick arrest of the culprits likely averted the formation of a mob.

En route to the visitation, I expected no more than a handful of people. Was I in for a surprise! More than 750 signed the register book!!

More surprises were on the way.

As I stood to conduct the service, I faced a standing room only crowd that packed the chapel of the funeral home.

The procession to the cemetery that ordinarily would have been escorted by one officer's vehicle was led by fourteen police cruisers with their bright, blue lights flashing. As we crossed the bridge over I-85, I said to my wife, "Folk passing through that don't know what is going on will assume President Bush has died and is being buried in Lanett."

B.J. never had many material possessions. The only time her name appeared in a newspaper was in the obituary column. But in terms of friends, she likely was the envy of many who live on "Silk Stocking Row".

She was sweet in disposition; in character, she was salt of the earth.

Circus

"Jim you've got to rescue us. Somebody failed to get a minister, and the service is at ten. Please tell me you can come." I explained it was already nine o'clock, I had not showered, and the funeral home was a thirty-minute drive from our house.

"I don't care how you smell, just get here as quickly as you can. It's a cremation so you won't have to go to the cemetery. And I'll tell you now, it will be different. This is an interracial, common-law, ticklish situation."

The sister of the deceased was the spokesperson in our hastily called session for planning the service. Whatever I might do, she would read the obit and when I learned there would be five (5) songs, all by Janis Joplin, she was designated to handle the music. Simple enough...and the husband was in full agreement...so we thought.

After the opening Scripture and prayer, the husband, holding six (6) red roses, rushes to the microphone and begins an unscheduled, eight-minute speech trying to reconcile with the deceased's parents and relatives who are seated on the front row rather than in designated family section. They sit like a line of Buddha's—arms folded, eyes closed and wearing angry scowls. When finished, he takes a seat by me on the podium rather than return to the family section. All the while, people were moving in and out, conversing as though they were at a carnival midway, a prophetic sign of more to come.

As the sister began the husband laid the roses aside and began making calls on his cell phone. When the sister introduced the last of the five songs, she laid heavy emphasis on this being the "VERY favorite" of the deceased. As the music started, the husband sprang into action. He stood, lifted his hands like a tent revival evangelist issuing an altar call, and in a loud voice said, "Joe! Charlie! Willie! Tom! Everybody! Karaoke! —to the words of "O Lord, Won't You Buy Me a Mercedes -Benz"!

I suddenly remembered the show-biz adage, "Never follow a dog act." But how could I avoid it? Knowing I would not be going to the cemetery, I gathered myself, approached the podium, read John 3:16-18, and quickly exited a side door and headed home.

Soon after my arrival home, the funeral director called and apologized for getting me into "this mess," and then said, "Would you believe..." Before she could speak further I interrupted her, "If it is about that service we just had, I will believe anything!" She explained the husband and a few cronies left the funeral home, went to the Cracker Barrel and became so disruptive the police had to be called.

She again apologized for involving me. "Really, Jeannine, you don't owe me an apology. I should thank you. You afforded me a front row seat to both a rock concert and a real-life show that would challenge Ringling Bros. and Barnum & Bailey. I didn't have to have a ticket, and I will get paid for it!"

Contrasts

"Today we are going to the country." The director was as good as his word. Interstate travel gave way to state highway, state highway gave way to farm-to market road, and that way gave way to an unpaved path that ran between the church and the burial ground.

The shiny new Cadillac hearse stood in sharp contrast to the mud-caked, dust covered dump truck parked beside it. Artistically etched in the glass of the hearses rear door was the corporate motto, "Dignity'. The front doors of the truck also carried an advertisement.

Possum White
Gravedigger

I remember when the funeral home in my home town replaced its Pontiac hearse with one made by Packard. And I remember when the Packard was replaced by a Cadillac. Though it was a used vehicle, Mr. Blakely, the local mortician, complained to me about the price of his new purchase. When I asked why he opted for a more expensive machine when cheaper brands were available, he explained it this way: "When I back my Cadillac up to the door of the poorest man in town, he is flattered. When I back up to the house of the richest man in town, he is not embarrassed. It is simply a matter of good public relations."

Dumb me. I had always thought the sole purpose of a hearse, whatever the emblem on its hood, was the safe transportation of the dead.

Someone said the Madison Avenue image-makers leave no stone unturned. Private mausoleums and fancy granite markers long have attested to that fact. Now we know their ubiquitous imprimatur also is stamped how we get there.

Comfort

The wife of a prominent, long-time Birmingham pastor died early on a spring morning. Burial would be in a family plot in south Alabama.

On Tuesday, several local ministers made their way to Evergreen to offer comfort to one who had comforted so many. Purposely arriving early to allow time for visiting, the group called on the family at the family home place... an old house with a neat yard and flowers blooming all over, which added to the beauty and serenity of the place.

Our friend graciously thanked us for our support and concern. Then he said something I will never forget. "You know, if what we believe as Christians is true, Easter Sunday is not a bad day to die."

We had gone to comfort him; we returned comforted by him.

Christmas Sorrow

On December 23, amidst the most joyous time of the year, I received one of the saddest phone calls of my life. "Jim, I've got an old lady here who is 86 years old. She's got no family, no friends, no money, no nothing. I am supposed to bury her in the morning at nine. I just don't feel right putting her in the ground without at least a prayer. Could you come?"

The early sky on Christmas Eve was overcast, gloomy and a light mist falling as if Mother Nature were on the verge of tears. With only the director and I present at the open grave with no tent overhead, no chairs for visitors to sit, no flowers — I read from Psalm 23 and John 14 and closed with a prayer.

Following the Christmas Eve service that night, our family gathered for a sumptuous holiday meal. After we ate, I hugged each of them a little tighter.

DR. JOHN: Scholar, Teacher, Farmer, Friend

John Haralson Hayes and I grew up in the same county, he in the country and I in town. Our families lived from pay day to pay day.

We were college-roommates. He taught me how to study and made sure I knew both the location and purpose of the library. Early in his student days at Howard College he was called as the "week-end warrior" pastor of a church in my hometown, Lanett, and I became the music director. We often worked as a team in youth and church revivals, but we never seriously challenged the fame or effectiveness of the Ira D. Sankey/ Dwight L. Moody or George Beverly Shea/Billy Graham duos. Later, on his recommendation, I would be called as pastor of his home church, Five Points Baptist.

From a high school graduating class of 12, he would finish academically first in his college class and be awarded a prestigious Fulbright Scholarship to the University of Edinburgh, Scotland. He completed his formal education with two degrees, including a Ph.D. from Princeton Theological Seminary. After 35 years on the faculty at Candler School of Theology he retired in 2007 as the Franklin Nutting Parker Professor of Old Testament. A world class scholar, his name appears on the spines of more than 40 books.

His last years were spent on a little farm only a stone's throw away from the one on which he was reared. When John failed to appear at the daily coffee session, a friend went the next day to check on his well-being. John had collapsed in the pasture, had laid there all night, and his body was covered with fire ants. That is not how he would have chosen to die, but he would have been pleased at the place of his demise, and to have breathed his last surrounded by the small herd of cows he loved so much.

His last public speaking likely was some four months earlier when he was the James A. Auchmuty Fund for Excellence in Congregational Leadership guest lecturer at Samford University and pulpit guest at Shades Crest Baptist Church that endowed the Fund and the church I served for 27 years.

I am grateful for the friendship we shared, the good times we enjoyed, and the doors he was instrumental in opening for me. Little did we know those few days in Birmingham would be our last together.

John well could have sat as the poster boy for the adage, it is amazing how far you can go if you keep on going.

Drugs: A Grave Issue

Two weeks earlier I had the service for an 18-year-old who hanged himself in jail. Facing charges for burglarizing a veterinarian's office in search of drugs was more than he could handle. His mother, an inmate at Tutwiler Prison for Women, was there in street clothes, accompanied by a guard. (For her to be present, the family had to pay the guard's regular pay for the day plus travel expenses.)

Now, the service for a 21-year-old who in a drug induced stupor attacked his father with a butcher knife. In turn, the father shot and killed him in what was ruled justifiable homicide.

The boy's younger brother was there dressed in prison clothes of broad black and white stripes, as if he were wearing the skin of an over-sized zebra. He, too, was accompanied by a guard.

Two years later, I chanced to meet the young man who had served his time.

"I know you" I said.

Surprised, he responded, "You do? How?"

I explained that I had conducted his brother's funeral and that I also knew his grandfather.

"Then you know how messed up my life was. I'm all straight now."

I shook his hand, told him how proud I was of and for him and added, "God bless you."

A month later I saw his grandfather in a place of business. I recounted my visit with his grandson and how happy I was for the boy and his family.

"He's dead" the grandfather said.

"Yeah, a couple of weeks ago he died of an overdose."

The life span of the average American is now 78 years. The combined lives of these two young men totaled 39 years. Tragically, these two will not be the last whose existence is cut in half by drugs.

Flexibility

Flexibility is the name of the game when it comes to funerals. Plans change at a moment's notice. Due to snafu's, neglect and various other good and bad reasons, more than once I have served as pallbearer, driver of the hearse and officiating minister on the same service.

"Oh, you're here for that funeral," the receptionist said as I approached her desk (as if I were just dropping in for a social visit and coffee with the staff).

"I am here for the two o'clock," I said.

"No, I mean the other one," she said.

"What other one? I don't know what you are talking about," I said.

The body of a man, dead at least a week, had been found and identified. His family, residing in metro New York City, who had not had contact with him in 7 years, wanted him cremated here and his ashes sent to them. And they wanted someone to "say the last rites" before the cremation.

The director carried me to an adjacent building that housed the cooler and crematory among other things. He punched in the security code, opened the door and we stepped inside the cooler, so named for good reason. There were 5 bodies awaiting cremation. As the director began moving gurneys to access the one in the corner in which we were interested, I asked what he was doing. "You do want to see him, don't you?" As in the case of Lazarus who had been dead for days (John 11) there was ample olfactory evidence of the presence of a corpse, and because of that no visual proof would be necessary. He then moved to the door and said, "Call me on your cell when you are finished." He was about to leave me alone in this eerie, dim-lit place. Or so he thought.

"Wait," I said, "we know nothing about this family, and they nothing about us. You know how litigious our society is. So, in the event there is a law suit, you will stay here as a witness that the last rites were conducted." I then read from the Scripture and had a prayer commending to God the spirit of this forgotten man and his family-

Outside in the fresh air warmed by the sun, and with few minutes left before the two o'clock service was to begin; I had a few minutes to reflect. This man had lived and died alone. There were only two people attending his "last rites," but I was aware of the Presence of Another in the smallest, most unusual "chapel" I had ever been in.

Family Feud

Today I would do double duty serving as both the minister and the assistant funeral director for this out of town service some forty miles away. My riding in the hearse saved me gasoline and it saved personnel expense for the mortuary.

No sooner than the director said to me, "We should be getting close," than my cell phone rang.

"Where are y'all?"

"I think we are in sight of the cemetery."

"Well, you may want to slow down. We just had a call that one family had just drawn a gun on another."

"Slow down nothing! Why do you think they make anti-lock brakes?"

Moments later we were greatly relieved to see two sheriff cars enter the cemetery. The culprit was arrested without incident and spirited away.

The brother who had been threatened explained today's "Misunderstanding" was but the latest in a series of incidents between him and his sibling. It was rooted, as so many family feuds are, in the issue of who is going to be in charge.

The service went without a hitch—until. When the locals digging the grave hit rock about two feet down, they simply moved over and started anew, leaving a much larger than normal hole. The director and I, anxious to "get out of Dodge," were delayed by having to help fill the grave.

Having spent most of this extended time anxiously looking over my shoulder and constantly looking in the rear-view mirror on the return trip, I got on a first name basis with a new friend, Ben Gay.

Funerals usually close with references to resurrection. This experience caused me to think perhaps there also should be an emphasis, at some point, on burying hostilities in the grave as well as coffins. Our emotional life would be healthier, family relationships would be happier—and the environment might be safer!

Face Card

Over the course of sixty-three years in ministry, I have buried people from all walks of life, some quite prominent "face cards" as the folk in my hometown called them. Among these high-profile individuals were leaders in finance, business, industry, education, government, and politics. But as far as fame goes, one stands head and shoulders above all the rest.

Her notoriety comes from association, but better borrowed glory than none at all. She was Lois Lane; no, not that one, another by the same name. If you are interested in researching her obituary, go to the archives of THE BIRMINGHAM NEWS rather than THE DAILY PLANET.

An Unclaimed Blessing

Lead times are so short for some funerals, some less than an hour that I feel as if I am an official member of the Minute Men. Not this time. The call came three weeks in advance including day, hour, and place.

The deceased, a never married woman, died out of state. Her relatives were so geographically scattered and their schedules so complicated that 21 days later was the first day they all could attend.

I was reminded of a story, perhaps apocryphal, of a spinster with no family who had taught school in a small community for 40 years. A loveable person, her contribution endeared her to everyone in town.

To insure she received proper recognition and respect due her, a committee of town folk paid a visit to the new editor of the county paper whose background was sports reporting. The group made it clear that he was to draft and print a worthy eulogy or else every subscription would be cancelled.

He never had drafted such a document, but he promised to do his best. The tribute in the next edition read:

> Here lie the bones of Nancy Jones.
> To her, life held no terror.
> She lived an old maid; She died an old maid.
> No hits, runs/no errors!

Since poems often are used at funerals, I thought, why not? But the higher angels of nature prevailed. Funerals are no place for Trivial Pursuit. And I did not wish to infuriate the family, embarrass myself, look for other employment or begin paying alimony.

Asian Mantra

No one needed to announce the arrival of the widow of the Chinese man who reportedly had worked as a dish washer at an Egg Roll Express. From the moment she exited the vehicle she began a loud, shrill mantra, "Ya! Ya! Ya!", which continued without interruption, throughout the entire service.

Immediately after the benediction I told the director, "I've got to find a place to be quiet for a few minutes. My head is splitting." He said she did the same thing when he had assisted her in planning the funeral. She made selections pointing to pictures and when he showed her the total bill she went, "YA! YA! YA!" She pulled out a large bundle of cash, paid the 5-figure bill and "the roll was still as big as cabbage."

Neither of us was ready to give up our day jobs, but we began reading the want ads for part-time dishwashing jobs at Chinese fast-food places.

A Rare Flash of Insight

John, a man in my home town who never was a Phi Beta Kappa candidate, reached his workplace potential as an elevator operator in the local textile mill. Pushing the Up or Down button and selecting the floor number to stop on wasn't exactly science but he showed a rare flash of insight at the time of his mother's death.

When his siblings met to discuss plans for the final disposition of their beloved dead, there was no question as to which funeral home, church, preacher and time of the service. Where she would be buried was the only unresolved issue.

John listened as his sister argued that Mama always wanted to be buried back up in the country in the cemetery of the church she attended as a youngster. His brother countered, arguing the matron's choice was burial in the local city cemetery. When they had their say, John broke his silence. His opening line infuriated the others, "Ya'll all are lyin'." The immediate, unspoken mental reactions were predictable: What does he know? And who is that dumb bunny to pass judgment on those of us who are so much smarter and successful than he? Then he spoke again after a pregnant pause, "Ya'll all are lyin'. The truth is, Mama never wanted to be buried."

Things Are Not Always as They Seem

Pursuant to his love for fishing, the treasurer of a church I once served bought a boat and trailer, a purchase of which he was more than proud. While washing his fiber glass beauty to a spit shine glow, he slipped, somersaulted to the ground and lay unconscious. His neighbor, a medical doctor, saw the whole episode from the window of his den. Before rushing to aid his friend, he called 911. One can only imagine the reaction of the dispatcher when she heard, "Man overboard on Chapel Road." Rather than discouraged by the incident, Barnacle Bill's appetite for a cabin on the water now was as intensified as that of a hungry wide mouth bass seeking minnows for breakfast.

Sometime later he phoned his daughter who lived in Mississippi, "Well, today I bought two lots on the lake." She was so happy one of her father's dreams had been fulfilled. "O Dad, I am so thrilled. Where is the place? Lake Martin, Logan Martin or Smith Lake?" she asked.

But her exuberance was as short-lived as a morning fog on a frog pond under a bright sun when he, in good Paul Harvey fashion, explained the rest of the story. "Neither, " he replied. "They are lots for your mother and me in Jefferson Memorial Cemetery. They are located on the backside of the place, just over the hill from a subdivision lake."

Above or Beneath the Sod

Sue and I had invited a cemetery counselor over to discuss arrangements for our funerals. Things went well until the subject of interment came up. "We offer traditional, in-ground burial, but perhaps you might be interested in above the ground entombment..." Had he stopped there we would have remained on good terms, but he added, *"like Jesus."* With that I became unglued. "Get real, man,": I said. "If they had backhoes back then he would have been put six feet under."

Yes, I over reacted. But I am possessed of a long-standing aversion to people who feel obligated to "speak the language of Zion" when conversing with a minister. To the surprise of many, including some men of the cloth, we are human beings like other folk. My over-sized ears can understand and prefer ordinary, down to earth conversation rather than contrived, artificially-adorned by religion, halo-encircled talk.

Quo Vadis?

The minister of music and I went by the funeral home to pay our respects to the longtime custodian of the church, the receptionist directed us to a door that led to the parlors. There the scene looked like rush-hour gridlock. Casketed bodies were lined up bumper to bumper in the hallway as well as the parlors. We finally located our friend as he "lay a corpse," as my grandmother would say, and having accomplished our mission, we prepared to leave.

Upon our exit the receptionist asked, "Did you find him all right?" With that, my co-worked bolted for the door while I remained to thank the lady for her help. Outside my sidekick was bent double with laughter. "What's so funny?" I asked. "Did you not hear what that receptionist said? She asked if we found him all right. We found him alright, but I don't know if he was all right or not. That's between him and the Lord."

When Heaven Becomes Hell

Constantly I encounter the idea that everybody automatically goes to heaven when they die. It matters not they never ever have made Jesus the Lord of their life, how they have lived or if God is only a swear word. Today would be a case in point.

The decedent would not be nominated as the denomination's Layman of the Year, but as is so often the case, folk try to make a person more in death more than they ever were in life. That role fell on the shoulders of the brother-in-law. He explained the decedent had his faults, had lived a rough life, was not "a religious man," never had joined a church, but "He was a believer, and that's all that counts."

Mentally I began to compare what I had just heard to what I had read in the Bible. Jesus spoke of heaven as a prepared place for a prepared people (John 14). The last book of the New Testament speaks of heaven being reserved for "only those who are written in the Lamb's book of life" (21:27). It is a place where archangels, angels, elders, martyrs and saints are preoccupied with the worship of God (4:1-22).

Given the contrasts described above, if people who never had a use for God on earth make it to heaven, rather than a place of blessing, heaven is going to be hell for them.

Block 30

Elmwood Cemetery in Birmingham, established in the early 1900's, is one of the largest in the South. Its 412 acres are divided into 50 blocks but Block 30 is unique.

You can follow the complex-encircling white or yellow stripes on the pavement to locate any grave in the expansive burying ground. However, a special red line abruptly stops at Block 30.

Of the 130,000 burials recorded at Elmwood, one in Block 30 stands out above the rest.

Thousands visit the graves of loved ones and friends, but one in Block 30 is the most visited of any.

However, the unpretentious granite marker on that special grave in Block 30 does *not* stand out from those around it. The names cut in the head stone are:

BRYANT

FOLMER

The foot stone is inscribed:

Paul William Bryant, Sr.
Sept. 11, 1913 - Jan. 26, 1983.

But for the red line and a few pieces of Crimson Tide memorabilia, you might drive right past it without realizing it as the final resting place of one of our state's most famous and revered citizens, The Bear.

Letting "Pass Away" Pass Away

The Living Bible, published in 1971, was one of many attempts to present the Bible in modern English. But were one published based on how we really *talk*, this what it may sound like:

Jesus suffered, bled and passed away

Through Jesus' passing away, burial and resurrection

Through his passing away on the cross

It is appointed unto man once to pass away

John 21:4 speaks of ""former things passing away," but where does Scripture say human beings "pass away"? We don't pass away, we die. And in dying, we transition to one of two new zip codes.

Using euphemisms is simply a way to avoid coming to grips with our own mortality. Experts remind us that until we can use the terms die, death and dying—all good Bible terms—we are in denial, simply playing mind games with ourselves. If a word (or words) is good enough for the Bible, it should be good enough for us. Therefore, let's let "pass away" pass away from our vocabulary.

www.ingramcontent.com/pod-product-compliance
Lightning Source LLC
Chambersburg PA
CBHW052148110526
44591CB00012B/1896